W9-CFF-359

Marketing and the Computer

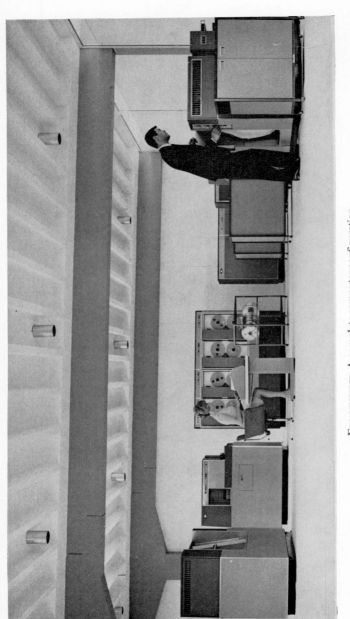

FRONTISPIECE. A complete computer configuration.

Marketing and the Computer

BY

I. St. J. HUGO

PERGAMON PRESS

OXFORD · LONDON · EDINBURGH · NEW YORK

TORONTO · SYDNEY · PARIS · BRAUNSCHWEIG

PERGAMON PRESS LTD.,
Headington Hill Hall, Oxford
4 & 5 Fitzroy Square, London W.1

PERGAMON PRESS (SCOTLAND) LTD.,
2 & 3 Teviot Place, Edinburgh 1

PERGAMON PRESS INC.,
44–01 21st Street, Long Island City, New York 11101

PERGAMON OF CANADA, LTD.,
6 Adelaide Street East, Toronto, Ontario

PERGAMON PRESS (AUST.) PTY. LTD.,
Rushcutters Bay, Sydney, New South Wales

PERGAMON PRESS S.A.R.L.,
24 rue des Écoles, Paris 5^e

VIEWEG & SOHN GMBH,
Burgplatz 1, Braunschweig

Printed in Great Britain by A. Wheaton & Co. Ltd., Exeter and London

08 103472 5 (flexicover)
08 203472 9 (hard cover)

Contents

Editors' Foreword to Series

THIS is a series of practical marketing handbooks written by British experts and designed as a library providing a compact and comprehensive review of modern marketing practice and technique.

The books are intended for sales and marketing managers, for marketing trainees and students of management, and for businessmen and managers of all kinds who are looking for an up-to-date, concise, readable statement of how the best British companies market their products.

Marketing as an accepted part of a business enterprise is a phenomenon of the last 10 years. Until then companies made goods and hoped that, by good fortune or through sales pressure, customers would be persuaded to buy them. As business has become more competitive, first in the consumer market and increasingly also in industrial markets, British managements have begun to appreciate the need for a rigorous and systematic approach to the market.

So much of the marketing approach seems obvious; it is surprising that the development of marketing thought and techniques should have spread so slowly through British industry. However, it is now possible to make a critical review of the best marketing practices in British industry. It is thus the purpose of this series to provide in simple terms descriptions and case studies demonstrating established techniques which can be used by the modern marketing executive to build for his company a strong position in the market and so make an important contribution to his company's profitability and contribute to the overall good of the community by ensuring that more and more people will be able to buy what they genuinely want and fewer customers will have to put up with second best.

The series has been so organized that, while each volume is self-contained, a connective thread runs through each so that the whole series will provide a compact and comprehensive review of marketing practice and techniques.

The editors would welcome at any time comments and criticism from their readers, and particularly suggestions for further additions to the range. The following titles are either available now or are in preparation:

Marketing Overseas
Marketing and the Brand Manager
Marketing through Research
Marketing and Financial Control
Marketing and the Computer

BERNARD TAYLOR
D. W. SMALLBONE

Editor's Foreword

THE phenomenon of the last 150 years of human progress has been the extension of man's muscle power through the development of machines.

It is probably true to say that the next 50 years will see an important revolution in the extension of man's brain-power through the development of computers.

One of the tragedies of the early years in computer development has been the inability of many managers to grasp the full importance of this new management tool.

So often the computer is regarded merely as a fast "quill pen", an extension of existing calculating equipment.

That it is, of course, but it is far more—it is a device fully capable of controlling and taking decisions across a whole range of situations.

Probably one of the most backward areas of computer development has been marketing. This book sets out to show the importance and versatility of the computer in marketing decision making.

Ashridge Management College   D. W. SMALLBONE
April, 1967

ix

Author's Preface

SUFFICIENT experience of computers in commerce has now been gained for their usefulness to be generally appreciated. The role of computers in commerce, however, is still far from being defined. There has been a tendency to timidity, understandable in view of users' unfamiliarity with the equipment, so that computers are frequently employed as no more than hyper-efficient calculating machines, performing largely accounting functions. Although computers can do such work well, and will no doubt continue to do it, their potential is being wasted if their work is limited to accounting.

With the relevance of computers to commerce established, and with an increasing number of personnel trained and experienced in their use, management can with confidence seek more sophisticated exploitation of computers' potential. An essential aid to the sophisticated use of computers has been the development of scientific management techniques. The use of these techniques would often be impractical were it not for the availability of a computer to perform repetitive and often complex calculations. Perhaps the most outstanding feature of computers is their ability to make decisions when these are reduced to simple logical steps. Scientific management techniques, by enabling management to explore the nature of complex decisions and thereby define what information is essential and how it should be treated, facilitate the use of computers in making such decisions.

Marketing decisions are frequently more difficult to make than decisions in other aspects of commerce, since information appertaining to markets is often rather vague. It is because of the sophisticated nature of marketing decisions that the use of computers in this field has been largely neglected. However, those companies that have used computers to help in making marketing decisions, particularly by providing up-to-the-minute information on the actual and potential market, have found their efforts well rewarded.

This book is intended for students of marketing and marketing personnel who have little or no experience of computers. The purpose of the book is to explain in lay language how computers operate and their capabilities, and then how computers can profitably be used in marketing. The book has the following structure:

PART I gives a brief outline of the development of computers and explains exactly what a computer consists of and how it works. There follows an account of the preparation involved in installing a computer and setting up a data processing department, with consideration of the re-organization of records and files.

PART II provides a brief explanation of the principles of some of the common scientific management techniques, and shows how a computer makes decisions.

PART III describes how the computer is used in the control of different aspects of marketing work.

PART IV has the same structure as Part III, but deals with more advanced and sophisticated use of the computer.

Acknowledgements

THE author would like to acknowledge all those who in any way contributed to making this book possible. In writing the book I received a great deal of valuable advice; the errors are my own. In particular, I must acknowledge the co-operation and encouragement received from International Computers and Tabulators Ltd., who were kind enough to waive copyright on many of the illustrations in this book, as well as allowing me access to their wealth of information on the subject treated.

Additionally, it would be ungrateful not to mention in particular C. Hampson-Evans, who provided the initial impetus to write this book, and subsequently a great deal of advice and criticism, and G. J. Mansell, another colleague in ICT, who contributed in a similar manner; and, finally, various members of Applications Development Division ICT, who also provided information and criticism.

The Computer

CHAPTER 1

A Brief History of Computers

THE history of the needs, ideas, and developments which have finally produced the modern electronic digital computer is as long as the history of arithmetic. It has been the need for greater speed and accuracy in computing, however, that has provided the principal impetus, and this need has been felt acutely only since the seventeenth century. From then on many scientists and mathematicians have applied themselves to the problem of producing a machine that could calculate both more quickly and more accurately than man. Prominent mathematicians have for centuries seen the benefits that would accrue to both science and commerce from such an invention and, as in the history of all inventions, have been constantly frustrated and thwarted by those with less vision than themselves. There have been many claims and counter claims to have invented the first true computer, but it is not the purpose of this chapter to enter into the argument. The following account confines itself to describing the major developments and some of the important contributors who have helped to produce the modern computer.

The first widely used computing machine was the abacus, a counting frame which is said to have been introduced into Europe about a thousand years ago. The abacus is still used to some extent today in the East, but although a skilled user can reach quite high speeds of calculation, it is limited by the need to be manually operated. During the reign of Elizabeth I, Francis Bacon revived the idea of binary arithmetic, an idea that was later taken up by Leibniz, but which was not to become really important until relatively recently. In 1642 Blaise Pascal built a simple calculating machine which was designed to be of use to his father in his work as a customs officer. Pascal's machine was manually operated, and used several wheels, each with ten teeth, one wheel representing units digits, another tens digits, and so on. The important innovation introduced by this machine was the provision of an automatic carry. In 1673 Leibniz designed a calculating machine called the "stepped wheel", but its operation was not always dependable. There were no more major developments until the beginning of the nineteenth century when Jacquard, in 1901, used punched cards to guide the operation of his looms. Jacquard himself was not concerned with the development of calculating machines, but a contemporary of his, Charles Babbage, was not slow to see that the same principles that Jacquard had applied to his looms could be applied to controlling and presenting numbers to calculating machines. Nearly a century was to elapse, however, before Jacquard's punched cards were applied in this way as a practical fact.

Charles Babbage (1792–1871) first conceived the idea of constructing a calculating machine when he was faced with sheets of logarithm tables which he knew to be full of errors. At this time all mathematical tables were produced by hand with a consequently high proportion of errors of calculation and transcription. Babbage realized that the best way to obtain accurate tables was to have them calculated mechanically, and, if possible, have the results printed by the calculating machine. He first directed his efforts at producing a difference engine, and managed to produce a small working model which he demonstrated in 1822. The model was received with enthusiasm, and Babbage then turned his attentions to constructing a larger machine for which he received financial support from the Royal Society and the Government. His backers underestimated the time and effort involved, however, and official support was withdrawn in 1842. Babbage's difference engine was abandoned until he had a chance to demonstrate it at the International Exhibition of 1862. It was subsequently used for computing life tables upon which insurance companies based their premiums for many years. In the meantime Babbage had conceived the idea of making an analytical engine, which he thought would be capable of performing any sort of calculation. Unfortunately he was unable to do more than produce a great many detailed drawings of its design from which it could have been made.

Babbage understood clearly what a computer would need to consist of. He knew that there would have to be mechanized means of feeding and extracting data, a store to hold data and instructions, an arithmetic unit to perform the calculations, and a control unit to control the operation of the machine. Babbage proposed to use punched cards as a means of input and output, and also as an auxiliary store. In order to overcome the problem of errors of transcription, he envisaged having the machine print out its results as an alternative form of output. He realized that a machine could not originate anything, since it could have no initiative; he also realized, however, that if a machine stored its instructions in mathematical form, it could be made to perform arithmetic on them, and thus modifiy them. The idea of a machine itself modifying its instructions is extremely important to the concept of modern computers. Unfortunately Babbage's vision could not be translated into practical terms because the necessary mechanical techniques were not then available. It is a measure of how far Babbage was ahead of his time that his inventions invalidated patents taken out as late as 1940.

Subsequent developments lacked the inspiration of Babbage, and it is only in recent years that his ideas have become practical reality. In 1885 William Burroughs produced the first adding machine, which he later developed to perform subtraction. The machine was operated by manually manipulated controls. An important step came when Dr. Hollerith, in 1890, introduced the first punched-card calculating system which worked electrically. This system was selected for use in the eleventh United States census. The particular importance of this invention lies in the use of punched cards and electricity. A significant development in the electrical field came in 1919 when Eccles and Jordan demonstrated that a thermionic valve could be in either of two stable states, and could be made to change from one to the other with the speed of light. This development does not seem to have been noticed by mathematicians of the day, perhaps because calculating machines at that time worked in denary arithmetic, whereas the significance of the development lay in its application to binary arithmetic. It was William Phillips who put this and other ideas together and who in 1934 produced a design for a simple electronic computer working in binary arithmetic.

Further progress was delayed at the start of the Second World War, although in the latter stages the introduction of new and complex weapons initiated the development of more powerful calculators to undertake the vast calculations with which scientists were faced. The development of computers further benefited from research into electrical pulses for the improvement of radar devices. In 1944 a calculating machine was made at Harvard which was capable of receiving input data, performing a sequence of calculations and recording the output; the speed of the machine was limited, however, by its partly mechanical structure. No completely electronic computer had yet been made at this time.

The first electronic computer was constructed at the University of Pennsylvania in 1946 and called the ENIAC. The electro-mechanical devices of previous machines were replaced by rapidly moving electrons which made calculations a thousand times faster than was possible before. This machine was still limited in concept, however, in that it was programmed by means of a plug-board, and had to be replugged every time that it was desired to change the program. The program could not be modified during operation. The operation of the machine was further complicated by the use of denary arithmetic.

The first stored program computer, the EDSAC, was made at Manchester University and became operational in 1949. This was really the first machine to include the basic principles that are embodied in the computers used today. This development was first commercially exploited in the UNIVAC 1 computer delivered to the United States Bureau of Census in 1951. In order for the use of computers to be feasible in commercial operations it was necessary to find a means of supplying the computer with data, and recording processed data, at extremely high speeds. Punched-card equipment in use at the time was adapted to fulfil this purpose, and high-speed printers were also developed to provide output information in readable form.

During the past 15 years developments have been rapid. The most fundamental developments include the introduction of paper tape and magnetic tape as cheaper and faster media for input and output, magnetic tape being used also as a cheap form of auxiliary store. More recent developments are the magnetic ink and optical character recognition systems which enable data recognizable to the human eye to be read into a computer, and the transmission of data keyed in on electrical keyboards from distant points connected by telephone or telegraph line to the computer. Storage units have been developed to permit the retention of vast quantities of data, using magnetic disc systems, or to permit rapid access to stored information using magnetic core storage. Finally, but most importantly, the introduction of transistors to replace valves greatly reduced the size and cost of equipment, and at the same time greatly increased its reliability.

Further developments occur almost daily, principally with respect to the speed at which data is processed. A further area of development is the automation of the operating of computers to an increasingly high degree, so that the amount of human intervention on the part of the computer operator is reduced to a minimum. In general, the cost of equipment is tending to fall, and methods of operating computers are becoming increasingly sophisticated. While technological breakthroughs cannot be precisely foreseen, general developments can; the possibilities appear almost limitless. They will remain possibilities, however, if developments are not taken advantage of and put to practical use. Enormous benefits could accrue to industry and commerce from the implementation of those techniques which exist already. Current developments are already years ahead of the practical applications to which they have been put, and the gap shows every sign of widening. The value of developments depends ultimately on their use, and that is up to commerce.

CHAPTER 2

What is a Computer?

A DISTINCTION may be made between two types of electronic computer—the analogue and the digital. In the analogue computer numbers are represented by some physical quantity such as length or electrical potential, and arithmetical operations are performed by making use of some law of physics. The accuracy of these machines is limited by the precision with which measurements are made, and high degrees of accuracy can be very expensive to obtain. Analogue computers are commonly used at present to control industrial processes, and may be ignored for the purposes of this book.

The digital computer represents numbers by patterns of magnetized material, and when associated with electro-mechanical peripheral devices will process data at extremely high speeds and output results in either coded form or in recognizable English and numerics. It is capable of carrying out all normal arithmetic functions and of making logical deductions on the basis of such calculations. The electronic digital computer is not capable of initiative; however, as Lady Lovelace said when writing of Babbage's engine: "It can do whatever we know how to order it to perform".

A digital computer normally comprises five basic units:

    (1) Input devices.
    (2) Output devices.
    (3) A store.
    (4) An arithmetic unit.
    (5) A control unit.

The input devices enable instructions and data to be read into the computer, where they are retained in some form of store until required. The control unit controls the operation of the series of instructions which constitute a program, and calls into play the input and output devices as they are required.

Logical or arithmetic calculations are performed in the arithmetic unit, and the output devices enable processed data to be output from the computer. These parts of a computer are known collectively as the "hardware"—the actual machinery.

In order for a computer to function, however, two other items are necessary—a program and data. The program is the series of instructions providing the directions to the computer which enable it to perform a particular job. The data is the information given to the computer on which the instructions are to be performed in order to produce the desired results. Programs, and the languages in which they are written, are collectively termed "software".

Hardware

It can be seen from the above description that the elements that make up a computer are essentially those that may be found in another form in any office. A secretary, for instance, receives information in her in-tray, or over the telephone, and transmits this information to her brain through her ears and eyes; her ears and eyes are her input devices. The secretary's brain is her control unit, telling her how to perform the various functions which must be carried out in order to complete a job. Her brain also forms part of her arithmetic unit and her store; information for immediate use is stored in her brain, but she also has a large reserve of information in filing cabinets. A hand adding machine is her arithmetic unit for long or complicated calculations. Her program is her knowledge of the job to be performed, and when she has performed it, she types out her results on her typewriter and leaves them in her out-tray. The typewriter and the out-tray are her output devices. This analogy, albeit somewhat simplified, should serve to dispel the disproportionate mystique surrounding computers.

Nevertheless, computers must be in some way exceptional to have created the degree of interest that is everywhere apparent today. The reasons for their importance may be summarized as follows:

(1) The ability to store vast quantities of information in a relatively small space.

(2) The ability to access this information at extremely high speeds.

(3) The ability to perform arithmetic and logical functions at extremely high speeds and with great accuracy.

(4) The ability to select and print out exactly the required information, without superfluities, at extremely high speeds.

In short, although a computer may perform no other functions than those that the secretary performs, it can do this on a scale and at a speed and accuracy far greater than can ever be achieved by human beings. As an example, an exchangeable disc store (Plate IX) can hold several million characters of information, letters, or decimal numbers, approximately the equivalent of 10–15 average-sized novels. Any items of information held in this store may be selected in under one-tenth of a second. Further details of the capabilities of computers are given in the appropriate sections in the detailed description of individual devices given below.

Input Media and Devices

In order for information to be acceptable to a computer the information which is to be input must be converted into a coded form. The code is known as a computer language (see p. 22). The coded information is then punched into either cards or paper tape, and read into the computer by means of a punched-card or paper-tape reader. The card or paper-tape reader accepts the information by detecting the pattern of holes punched into the input medium according to the code used. The card reader illustrated (Plate VI) can read 900 cards per minute. *Punched cards* are usually of a standard 80-column size, and may be prepared by means of an automatic key punch; they may be verified by sensing the holes using a similar keyboard. They provide a cheap and easily manipulated form of data storage, although they can prove bulky if the volume of data is large. High-speed reproduction of cards is possible, and they can be sorted, collated, and tabulated on ancillary equipment. Their use as computer input can help to provide an easy transition to working with a computer system for companies which already have punched-card equipment. Punched cards may also be prepared as output from the computer (see below, Output Devices).

Paper tape may also be prepared by the use of a key punch similar to that used for preparing punched cards. The tape is then verified by punching a second tape and comparing the two. One of the advantages of paper tape is that it can be prepared as a by-product of other functions; some electric typewriters and keyboard accounting machines, for instance, can produce a punched paper tape which can be assumed to be correctly punched if the figures thrown up by the accounting machine or typewriter are correct. Paper tape may also be incorporated into a teleprinter circuit, and thus provides a convenient means of transmitting data over distances in a form acceptable to computers. Paper tape provides a less bulky form of storage than punched cards, but is not as easily manipulated. Paper tape may also be prepared as output from the computer (see Output Devices). Tape readers can transfer up to 1000 characters per second as input.

Although punched cards and paper tape are the principal media for input to the computer, they have the disadvantage of holding data in a form which is not readily intelligible to human beings. Research has therefore been directed to finding some form of input which would be easily recognized by both the computer and human beings, and has resulted in the development of *optical* and *magnetic ink character recognition* techniques (Fig. 1). The magnetic ink character reader can be used to sort, verify, and read into the computer documents which have data imprinted on them in a special ink in a specific location. The reader recognizes data by sensing the pattern of ink. The characters are sometimes stylized, as can be seen in Fig. 1, in order to aid their recognition. A particular use of this equipment is in the processing of cheques.

(a)

(b)

FIG. 1. The E13B fount for magnetic ink character recognition.

The optical character reader works on a similar principle to the magnetic ink character reader, except that it recognizes characters by means of reflected light from a pattern of black ink and white paper which together forms a character. This technique has been developed less than the magnetic ink character recognition technique.

Output Media and Devices

As has been indicated in the previous section on input devices, two output devices are the *card punch* and the *paper-tape punch*. These devices punch data into cards and paper tape in the same way as the key punches, except that their operation is controlled by the computer and is therefore many times faster than the manually operated punches. A card punch on-line to the computer can punch 350 cards per minute, and a paper-tape punch 110 characters per second. Computer output is generally required to be readily recognizable to the human eye, however, and since this is not the case with punched cards and paper tape, this form of output is more convenient when it is to be input to the computer again.

Paper tape is sometimes used to operate an electric typewriter and produce typed output or, as suggested earlier, for input to transmission devices.

Most printed output is produced on the *line printer* (Plate V). This is a tabulator type of printing unit which prints a whole line of up to 160 characters of data at a time. Although the line printer receives information in coded form, the printed output is in readable form. Some line printers can print over 1,000 lines per minute.

Two less common output devices are the visual display unit and the digital plotter. The *visual display unit* (Plate VIII) consists basically of a cathode ray tube and an associated keyboard. Requests for information held in the computer are keyed in on the keyboard and the requested information is displayed visually on the screen. It is possible to obtain not only numeric and alphanumeric information but also graphical co-ordinate points and vectors. The *digital plotter* provides a means of representing numerical information in graphical form. The paper on which plotting takes place is wound on two rollers and passes over a rotatable plotting drum, over which is mounted a pen carriage. The pen and drum move independently to record graphically streams of data characters transferred to the plotter.

A further device which must be mentioned is the *interrogating typewriter*. This is an electric typewriter which may be used either for keying in information to the computer or for extracting information from it. It is not used for inputting or outputting large volumes of data, but merely to answer brief queries or add short items of data.

The Store

It is necessary to differentiate between two types of store; immediate access store (IAS) usually referred to as magnetic core store, and backing store. Immediate access store forms part of the central processor of the computer, and since it is expensive, only a limited amount of this type of storage is usually available. Access to information held in IAS is extremely rapid since no moving parts are involved, all operations being carried out electronically. This store is therefore used to hold data currently being processed and the instructions governing the processing.

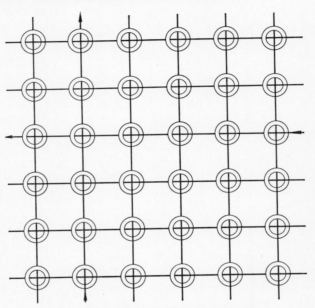

FIG. 2. Example of a magnetic core matrix.

Magnetic core store consists of a pack of very small rings, or cores, of ceramic material impregnated with magnetizable ferrous oxide and strung on wires in a frame, as illustrated in Fig. 2. Each core represents a binary digit, or "bit", and the total number of cores in the store is divided into groups of cores which form the unit of storage for a particular machine. The unit of storage is usually known as either a "byte" or a "word", the former consisting commonly of eight bits and the latter of twenty-four, although the unit of storage may consist of any number of bits that the manufacturer decides is appropriate to a particular machine. The size of core store is referred to in thousands of words or bytes, a thousand being represented by the symbol K; thus a 16K computer is one that has 16,000 words or bytes of core store. Modern computers are not generally available with less than 4K words of core store, and may have much more. Although magnetic cores are the usual form of IAS in new machines sold in the mid 1960's, other forms of immediate access store are available.

The *backing store* is used to hold essential data which is required only at relatively infrequent intervals and need not, therefore, occupy valuable space in the more expensive core store. There are two principal kinds of backing store categorized according to the degree of accessibility of data held on them: these are direct access storage and serial access storage. As the terms imply, items of data held on direct access storage can be accessed directly no matter where they are within the store, whereas items held on serial storage can only be accessed by reading all preceding items in the sequence in which they are held. Locating items of data held on direct access storage is therefore faster in principle; direct access storage devices are, however, more expensive than serial access devices. Direct access devices are therefore used most frequently when it is required to gain rapid access to individual items from amongst a large volume of data. An instance of such a requirement is an airline ticket reservation whereby requests for reservations are received from distant points connected by data transmission links to the computer, and these requests, which may apply to any one of the airline's flights on any date, must be satisfied immediately. Serial storage devices, on the other hand, are most frequently used to hold information which must in any case be accessed in large volumes or serially. Instances of such information are programs, in which instructions are obeyed in sequence, and most commercial data such as customer accounts files, in which records will normally be held in account number sequence, and the whole file processed at regular intervals rather than individual records processed when transactions occur.

Two principal direct access storage devices are the magnetic drum and the disc store. The *magnetic drum* consists of a large revolving drum, coated with magnetizable material, which is divided into peripheral bands. The bands pass under read and write heads which extract or feed in information. A magnetic drum can hold over 2 million characters of information, and items of data can be accessed in microseconds.

The *disc store* consists of a number of discs coated with magnetizable material which revolve on a central cylinder. Read and write heads are positioned above and below each disc, both surfaces of the disc being used, and as the discs revolve the heads can move across them to retrieve or write information. Discs can be fixed or a given number of discs can be contained in a cartridge which is interchangeable. A cartridge of six discs can hold several million characters of information, and since the cartridges are interchangeable the amount of data that can be stored in this way is virtually limitless. Moreover, an item of data held on discs can be accessed in an average time of some milliseconds.

Because of the higher cost of direct access devices, serial storage is often used instead. Moreover, if the information stored has in any case to be retrieved sequentially, no great advantage may be obtained by the use of direct access devices. The principal form of serial storage is magnetic tape. *Magnetic tape units* (Plate IV) work on a similar principle to the domestic tape recorder, though at very much greater speeds. Reels of magnetic tape pass under read and write heads by means of which data is stored or retrieved.

As many as 800 characters can be stored on one inch of magnetic tape. The time taken to access any given item of data depends on the length of tape preceding its location, since all data must be retrieved in sequence. However, data can commonly be transferred to or from tape at a rate of 60,000 characters per second, and even higher transfer rates are possible.

All the devices described as backing store may also be considered as input and output devices, since information is transferred between them and the immediate access store in the central processor. It is general practice to hold all repeatedly used programs and frequently used data, such as files, permanently on some form of backing store and to read these into the immediate access store when they are required.

However, all information must originally be read into a computer via one of the devices described in the section on input before it can be written to the backing store. Therefore, although backing store devices can input information which has already passed through the central processor, they cannot input original information. For this reason backing store devices have not been considered in the section on input devices.

The Arithmetic Unit

The arithmetic unit forms part of the central processor of the computer. All arithmetic and logical functions are performed in this unit, and since they are performed in binary arithmetic, to which references have previously been made, it is as well that this method of calculation should be clearly understood. Binary arithmetic is so called because numbers are constructed on a base of 2, just as decimal numbers are constructed on a base of 10. Whereas decimal numbers have columns for units, tens, hundreds, thousands, and so on, binary numbers have columns for the unit 1, and then successively for 2, 4, 8, 16, and so on. Displacing decimal digits by one column to the right or left will multiply or divide the number by 10; similarly, displacing binary digits by one column to the right or left will halve or double numbers. Numbers are represented in binary notation by a series of 0's and 1's; a 1 indicates that the value of that column is included, a 0 that it is excluded. Binary notation is illustrated in Table 1.

TABLE 1

Value of column	32	16	8	4	2	1	Decimal equivalent
		1	0	1	1	1	23
	1	1	0	0	1	1	51

A table of decimal numbers and their binary equivalents is given in Table 2.

TABLE 2

Decimal	Binary	Fraction
100	1100100	
10	1010	
9	1001	
8	1000	
7	111	
6	110	
5	101	
4	100	
3	11	
2	10	
1	1	
0.9375	0.1111	$\frac{15}{16}$
0.875	0.111	$\frac{7}{8}$
0.75	0.11	$\frac{3}{4}$
0.625	0.101	$\frac{5}{8}$
0.5	0.1	$\frac{1}{2}$
0.375	0.011	$\frac{3}{8}$
0.25	0.01	$\frac{1}{4}$
0.125	0.001	$\frac{1}{8}$
0.0625	0.0001	$\frac{1}{16}$

Using binary representation, all arithmetic can be carried out by means of the logical functions AND, OR, and NOT. Circuits called "gates", which are contained inside the arithmetic unit, perform these three functions. Each gate has one or two input lines and one output line. An AND gate will emit an output pulse only if pulses are received on both input lines. This gives rise to the following results expressed in binary digits:

$$1 + 1 = 1$$
$$1 + 0 = 0$$
$$0 + 1 = 0$$
$$0 + 0 = 0$$

An ʳOR gate will emit an output pulse if pulses are received on either one or both of the input lines, giving the following results:

$$1 + 1 = 1$$
$$1 + 0 = 1$$
$$0 + 1 = 1$$
$$0 + 0 = 0$$

A NOT gate will emit an output pulse if no pulse is received on the input line; if a pulse is received on the input line, no output pulse will be emitted. Thus this gate effectively changes the value of whatever is input to it, producing the opposite value.

Thus
$$0 = 1$$
$$1 = 0$$

By combinations of these logical functions it is possible to perform on binary numbers all the arithmetic operations of add, subtract, multiply, and divide.

Binary arithmetic is employed in computers because numbers are easily represented and manipulated in this form. Electronic devices can be rapidly switched from one state of magnetization to another or, in binary representation, 1 to 0. When punched cards or punched-paper tape is read by a card or tape reader, the pattern of holes in the input medium is represented by corresponding patterns of magnetization in the computer. Since each bit can be in either of two states of magnetization, any two consecutive bits provide $2 \times 2 = 4$ possible patterns; similarly, three consecutive bits prove $2^3 = 8$ possible patterns, and so on. Six consecutive bits provide 64 possible patterns, and if each of these states is taken to represent a different symbol, the six bits can be made to represent the ten decimal digits, 0–9, all the letters of the alphabet, and several other symbols such as plus, minus, and punctuation marks. Thus not only can arithmetic be performed in the binary code, but alphabetic and other symbols can be compared and manipulated in the same way that numbers can. It is thus possible to perform the functions of sorting, collating, and filing of alphabetic items on the computer.

The Control Unit

The control unit is also situated within the central processor of the computer, and is the device which translates the instructions contained in the program into action. (It will be remembered that the program is the series of instructions defining the task that the computer is to perform.) Each instruction consists of an operation to be performed, and the location of the information concerned in the operation; the location in which the result of the operation is to be placed may also be specified or it may be implied. The control unit is basically a multi-portion switch whose setting is modified by the instruction being carried out, thus activating the appropriate electrical circuits to carry out the operation, and accessing the specified storage locations.

Modern computers usually have a special control program, which is held permanently in core store, and given some name such as Executive, Monitor, or Supervisor. The principal purpose of this supervisory program is to aid in the efficient running of programs; its functions may include, to control transfers of data between the central processor and peripheral devices, to provide a means of communication between the central processor and the computer operator, and to control multi-programming activities. Multi-programming is the term given to the concurrent running of more than one program which can be achieved on large machines. When a program requires to use a peripheral device, it makes a request to the supervisory program. The supervisory program will check that the requested peripheral device is available, initiate the transfer, and then select another program to use the now momentarily freed central processor. In this way the most efficient use of equipment is ensured.

Communication between the central processor (Plate X) and the computer operator is achieved via the supervisory program, as mentioned above, and either a switch panel or, more usually, a console typewriter (Plate II). An example of a typical communication between the operator and the central processor would be the following. A program using the central processor encounters an error and transfers control to the supervisory program. The supervisory program activates the console typewriter to type out a message in a predetermined code indicating to the operator the type of error encountered. The operator then types in an instruction requiring the supervisory program to take some appropriate action to correct the error or ignore it, as the case may be, and allow the program which encountered the error to continue. If a control panel is in use instead of a console typewriter, the error will be indicated to the operator by a pattern of lights; the operator instructs the supervisory program on what action to take by setting a pattern of switches.

Software

Software is the term given to those facilities, other than the physical equipment and the supervisory program (hardware), which are essential to the operation of a computer. The term is sometimes extended to include personnel who work with the computer and facilities for training them, but for the purposes of this chapter will be limited to include only programming languages and programs.

A program may be described as the series of instructions by means of which the task to be performed is presented to the computer. A task is broken down into a series of simple logical steps all of which are included in the repertoire of operations built into the computer. Each different operation is represented inside the machine by a numerical code which is known as the machine code. When the series of instructions has been written, it is punched into cards or paper tape and read into the computer. The data on which the operations are to be performed is also punched into cards or paper tape, and as it is read in, the computer starts to select and obey instructions one by one in the sequence in which they are placed in the program. "Jump" instructions are provided so that the purely sequential performing of instructions may be temporarily discontinued. Where a short series of instructions needs to be performed several times in one program, the series, termed a "subroutine", need be written only once and can be held outside the main sequence; a jump can be to the subroutine at appropriate points in the program. When this series of instructions has been performed, a jump is made back to the main program at the instruction following the original jump instruction. Instructions in the program will then continue to be performed sequentially until another jump instruction is encountered.

Programming Languages

Just as people have a native tongue, so for each type of computer there is a specific language through which it operates, called its machine code. When it is desired to communicate information to a machine, there arises the question of how best to do this. Obviously, people do not habitually use machine code, and neither can machines "understand" human languages, so that a compromise is necessary. The alternatives are either to instruct people in machine code or else to find some method of making human language, or something resembling it, acceptable to the machine. Both of these alternatives have been implemented, producing three levels of language. Machine code is considered to be the lowest level, while languages nearest to those used by people are considered to be the highest, and are called autocodes. Assembly languages form a compromise between these two levels.

Assembly languages were first devised to make programming easier by allowing the programmer to use a code with a more immediately recognizable meaning than the purely numerical machine code. Typical assembly language and machine code instructions are contrasted in Table 3.

It is clearly easier for a programmer, when he wishes to instruct the machine to add, subtract, or multiply, to write ADD, SBT, or MPY rather than 001, 003, or 040. Each computer, or series of compatible computers, has a suitable assembly language devised

TABLE 3

Assembly language instructions			Machine code instructions		
ADD	UNIT	TOTB	001	4791	2369
MPY	TOTB	WTX	040	2369	1043
DVD	NETA	MTHS	044	3498	3690
SBT	TOTC	TOTB	003	2481	2369
PRI	TOTB	LINE	071	2369	5611

for it by the machine manufacturer. Programmers use the assembly language to write their instructions, called the source programs, but the machine can operate only in its own machine code. The computer is therefore provided with a special program, called an assembler, by which it converts the assembly language instructions into machine code. The source program is read into the computer and processed as though it were data by the assembler to produce the corresponding machine code instructions, or object program as they are called. The object program can then be used to perform the task that is required.

A limitation of assembly languages is that they can be used only on the computers for which they were devised. Thus whenever a different make of computer was encountered, either because the programmer changed jobs or because the company changed computers, the programmer had to learn a different assembly language, or the company had to have new programs written. It was therefore desirable to have some languages which were compatible with many or all machines, so autocodes were devised. Instead of being oriented towards specific machines, as are assembly languages, autocodes are oriented towards specific types of applications, and can be used on most or all machines. COBOL (Common Business Oriented Language), is the name of an autocode particularly suitable for programs written to perform commercial tasks, although this does not preclude its use for programming other work. Similarly, FORTRAN (FORmula TRANslation), and ALGOL (ALGOrithmic Language), are mathematical autocodes particularly suitable for technical and scientific applications. Just as with assembly languages, it is necessary to have a special program to convert source programs written in an autocode into machine code instructions. The special program that converts autocode into machine code, however, is called a compiler. Compilers for most of the widely used autocodes are provided by the machine manufacturers. Since autocodes need reflect the characteristics of no particular computer, they can be made to resemble closely the terminology used by human beings. This can be seen from the autocode instructions illustrated in Table 4.

TABLE 4. AUTOCODE INSTRUCTIONS

FORTRAN	REAL FUNCTION AREA (A, B, C),	
	$S = (A + B + C)/2.0$	
	AREA = SQRT (S *(S–A) * (S–B) *(S–C))	
COBOL		
	SALES–COMMISSION.	IF SALES IS GREATER THAN QUOTA GO
		TO FORMULA –2, MULTIPLY SALES BY 0.02
		GIVING COMMISSION. GO TO CONTINUE.

It is evidently easier for a programmer to use an autocode to write instructions than for him to use an assembly language. Because autocodes are not oriented towards the computer, however, the object program that is produced is often less efficient as regards processing time than one produced using an assembly language.

A great advantage gained from the use of assembly language and autocodes is the automatic allocation of data storage areas. Programmers writing in machine code had to allocate items of data to specific storage locations, represented by a number (see Table 3), and had to remember in which location they had placed that data. The use of higher level languages, however, permits the programmer to give storage areas a name which can be easily remembered. The item "gross pay", for instance, might be given a location with the name GROSS or GPAY. This is far easier for the programmer to remember than, say, 3179. The item of data will, in fact, have a location number, but this is allocated by the compiler or assembler and need not concern the programmer. Every time that a reference is made in the program to the storage location GROSS, the compiler or assembler will automatically substitute the location number which it has allocated to this area as it compiles or assembles the object program. This facility relieves the programmer of the tedious task of having to allocate numbered storage areas, remembering what is stored there, and avoid duplicating areas. All this is taken care of by the compiler or assembler.

Special Purpose Programs

Machine manufacturers provide not only the programming languages and assemblers and compilers, which are essential to the running of a computer, but also certain programs to perform specific tasks common to all or large groups of users. Programs supplied to the user in this way can be divided into several categories.

There are, firstly, subroutines for the input and output of data and for the validation of input data and the editing of output data. These sort of subroutines are often known collectively as "housekeeping", since they are concerned with the rather mundane function of getting data into the computer and in a form in which it is ready for processing, or out of the computer in the format that the user requires. All users will require to use these subroutines, and since writing them involves close attention to detail, errors are easily made. This is avoided by the machine manufacturer supplying standard subroutines which have already been tested for errors, so that the user's programmers are relieved of a great deal of tedious work.

A second category of subroutines is provided for technical and commercial calculations common to most users. These subroutines perform such functions as the calculation of sine, cosine, tangent, square root, and so on, and will clearly be used frequently in mathematical or engineering operations. Commercial subroutines provided perform the calculation of tax and social security deductions from gross pay.

Apart from these short routines, larger software "packages" are provided to perform more complex operations. One group of these packages is concerned with the manipulation of large volumes of data. It is frequently necessary to sort data to a particular sequence; orders, for instance, may need to be sorted first to product type sequence, and then to customer account number sequence. Routines to perform a variety of sorts are available. Larger packages are also available for information retrieval and indexing, both functions being useful in setting up files and retrieving volumes of a specific type of data from them.

Finally, there are the large commercial and technical packages. The importance of these packages to the user cannot be too greatly stressed, since their availability can make the difference as to whether a process is run on the computer or not. The large packages cover such commercial processes as inventory and production control, and provide for the use of the PERT control technique. The mathematical packages cover linear programming, statistical analysis, and provide large models for management games. The effort involved in producing these software packages is considerable, and many users would not be able to afford to write the necessary programs themselves. Thus if these packages were not made available to the user by the machine manufacturer, many processes which the user can now computerize comparatively cheaply would prove too expensive. In this case, the computer might well be used as an efficient and rather exotic calculator to perform clerical and accounting functions and nothing more. This would be a tragic waste of the computer's potential, for it is by the use of a computer in conjunction with scientific management techniques that the true worth of a computer can be realized.

Moreover, many of the more complex problems to which scientific techniques are now applied could not be solved economically without the speed and accuracy in processing that a computer provides. Modern techniques of management and computers are thus complementary, and since software packages are available to perform a variety of commercial and technical processes using these techniques, users are able to take advantage of them without the expense of programming them themselves.

CHAPTER 3

Installing a Computer

THE delivery of a computer may be regarded as the first step in a new phase of development for the company; it is also the culmination of possibly as many as three or more years of intensive effort. It is the purpose of this chapter to indicate some of the main areas and ways in which this effort has to be expended before a computer can become operational within a company. Before an order is placed with a computer manufacturer there should have been a feasibility study in the company concerned to establish the viability of a computer project, to determine the areas of work that could profitably be computerized, and to estimate what savings or benefits should be realized. In this chapter it will be assumed that a feasibility study has already been made, and that it has been decided to install a computer which will have a wide variety of applications in the company's work.

The Data Processing Department

The company will need a new department to organize and prepare work which is to be processed on the computer and to control the operation of the computer. This department is usually known as the data processing (DP) department, since it is the function of the computer to process data. The department will comprise a data processing manager, systems analysts, programmers, operators, and a number of clerical grade staff for such tasks as punching, verifying, and collating data. The functions of all these personnel are explained later in the chapter.

A point of immediate concern is the position of the DP depart-ment within the departmental structure of the company. If the DP department is to process the work of various other departments without bias to any one, and to be seen to do this, it must not come under the jurisdiction of any of the other divisions of the company. On the other hand, it must be at such a level as to permit easy and frank communication between itself and the departments to which it is providing a service. The concept of data processing as a

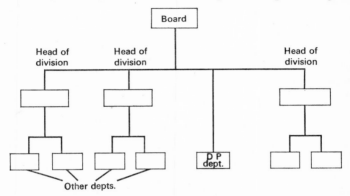

Fig. 3. Position of the DP department within a company.

service is important; any attempt to impose computerization on departments will in the long run meet with frustration. This point is dealt with more fully later in the chapter. A solution which meets the above requirements is to have the DP department on a working level with the departments it serves, but outside the main departmental structure of the company and reporting directly to a senior executive responsible at board level, for data processing. This is illustrated in Fig. 3.

Functions of DP Personnel

Very soon after the computer has been ordered a start will have to be made on selecting personnel for the DP department. A number of DP staff may be recruited from within the company, in which case time will have to be allowed for their training. Some staff experienced in data processing will, however, have to be recruited from outside the company.

The manager of the DP department will usually be recruited from outside the company since he will need previous experience of electronic data processing. The DP manager will be responsible for the efficient running of the DP department when it becomes operational, and for liaising with other departments whose work is processed on the computer. Initially, the DP manager will help to select and train the other personnel who will work in the DP department; he will also organize the preparations for installing the computer, including the conversion of systems and files.

The next staff to be recruited are the systems analysts. The series of procedures by which data is processed in order to obtain the desired information is known as a system. A computer system involves documents, people, and the computer, and it is the job of the systems analyst to form an efficient system from these three components. The systems analyst starts by investigating the existing procedures. He first establishes the objectives of the work he is investigating, and keeps these aims constantly in mind. He then obtains copies of all documents that are used, ascertains their purpose, who sees them and why, and traces their passage through the various departments. He interviews personnel to gain an understanding of their jobs and to determine what information they require, and whether they are currently receiving insufficient or superfluous information. All this information is recorded and classified by the analyst so that when he has found out what he needs to know, he can analyse it and determine what changes need to be made to produce a system compatible with the use of a computer.

All this work is preparatory to the design of the new computer system. When designing the new system, the analyst bears in mind such tenets of his trade as, "documents are necessary evils" and "the ultimate simplification is elimination". Nevertheless, it may be necessary to design new forms to replace unsuitable ones. It will certainly be necessary to establish new procedures for working.

Perhaps the hardest part of the systems analyst's job is to gain acceptance of the new system. This is usually best done by getting personnel at all levels involved in the systems investigation, so that, in fact, the personnel who will have to operate the system design it themselves with the guidance of the systems analyst. The worth of a systems analyst depends ultimately not on what he finds out or designs, but on what he manages to get implemented. When an acceptable new system has been produced, the systems analyst writes out a complete description of it, called a systems definition, and the system is then frozen. Any subsequent amendments to the system have to be made through a specified procedure and with the authority of certain appropriate senior staff.

Systems analysts will require a knowledge of computers, an understanding of a company's methods of working, and a sympathetic personality. Analysts may be recruited both from within and outside the company, those recruited internally having a greater appreciation of the company's methods of working, while those recruited externally would be required to have a sound knowledge of data processing. The number of analysts engaged will depend on the amount of systems work to be done. If more than three are engaged it is usually beneficial to divide them into teams and to appoint a senior analyst to allocate projects, and co-ordinate and control systems work. If only one or two analysts are employed this work can be done by the DP manager.

Shortly after the systems analysts are engaged, programmers will need to be recruited. Basically programming involves breaking down the task to be performed into a series of logical steps and then encoding these steps in a computer language so that the computer can perform the required task. In the systems definition the systems analyst will have laid down in outline the way in which each of the jobs to be processed on the computer is to be performed. This broad method of approach will be illustrated by a block diagram, such as the one shown in Fig. 4.

The programmer uses the block diagram and the accompanying narrative in the systems definition to draw up a flowchart which illustrates the job in more detail, indicating input and output

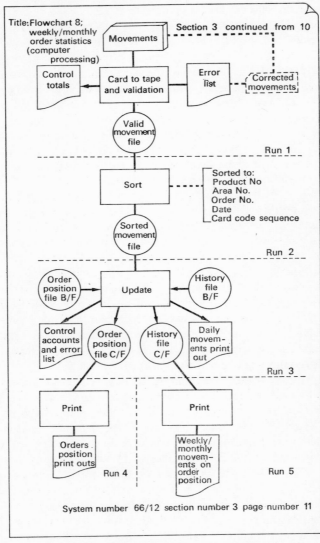

Title: Flowchart 8; weekly/monthly order statistics (computer processing)

Section 3 continued from 10

Movements

Control totals ← Card to tape and validation ← Error list ← Corrected movements

Valid movement file

Run 1

Sort — Sorted to: Product No / Area No. / Order No. / Date / Card code sequence

Sorted movement file

Run 2

Order position file B/F → Update ← History file B/F

Control accounts and error list / Order position file C/F / History file C/F / Daily movements print out

Run 3

Print / Print

Orders position print outs   Run 4

Weekly/ monthly movements on order position   Run 5

System number 66/12 section number 3 page number 11

Fig. 4. Sample flowchart showing computer runs.

functions, and record handling and comparison. If the job is at all complicated it may be necessary to produce detailed flowcharts which break the job down into even smaller steps corresponding to three or four program instructions. All illustrations are marked with numerical and literal cross-referencing symbols. Examples of flowcharting are given in Figs. 5 and 6. The step represented by

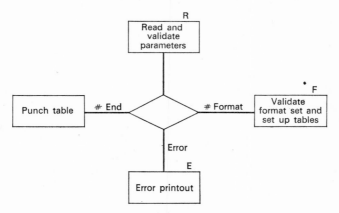

FIG. 5. Outline program flowchart. This outline flowchart shows a card validation routine. The cards are read, individual parameters validated, and a check made to ensure that the correct number of cards are present (format). When an "end" card is encountered, a a table of the data held on preceding cards is printed. Any errors encountered in the validation checks cause a branch to an error routine.

symbol E in the outline flowchart is broken down into a detailed flowchart. The flowcharts are drawn using standard symbols. What symbols are used is less important than that they should be standarized to facilitate comprehension of the flowchart.

When flowcharting has been completed, the programmer writes instructions in the selected computer language and accompanies this with narrative so that what he is doing can be readily recognized without constant recourse to the less intelligible program instructions. Once the program has been written it has to be

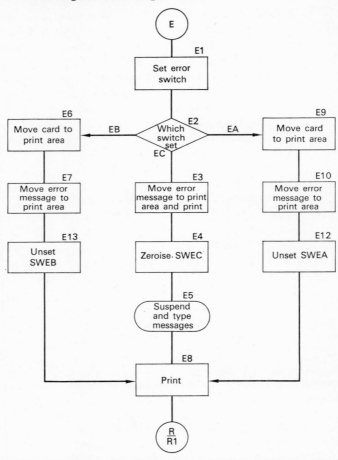

FIG. 6. Detailed program flowchart. The error printout routine shown in Fig. 5 is here considered in detail. A switch is set according to the type of error encountered. This causes a branch to be made to one of three routines, each of which causes an appropriate message to be printed out, and sets the switch ready for the next error. In one case (EC) the type of error is serious enough to prevent the program continuing; a message is therefore typed out on the console typewriter, and the program is suspended waiting for some action to be taken by the computer operator.

checked visually and then tested for errors on the machine, using test data specially prepared by the programmer to test all the conditions that the program is likely to encounter. This error checking procedure is sometimes known as "debugging", and is vital if programs are to run efficiently when applied to proper "live" jobs.

Programmers can often be recruited from inside the company, usually on an approximate ratio of two to one to the systems analysts. It is generally advisable to engage at least one experienced programmer from outside the company so that he can help to supervise the work of trainees. There will in any case have to be a senior programmer to allocate work to the other programmers and control their efforts, unless the number of programmers is very small, in which case a systems analyst might undertake this supervisory role.

When a program has been written and visually checked, it has to be punched into either cards or paper tape before it can be run on the computer. There is, therefore, a requirement for punch and verifier operators. In fact there are many other tasks which may be included under the general heading of data preparation. Great use is made of codes to classify data to be processed on the computer, so that coding staff will be required. There is a need for very tight control of all data to be processed, so that staff will be required to be responsible for the receipt and dispatch of data, and for checking control totals. Ancillary equipment may be used for sorting, collating, decollating, and tabulating, in which case ancillary machine operators will be required. All these staff can be recruited from within the company; comptometer operators, for instance, can be retrained as punch and verifier operators.

Once a job has been prepared for input to the computer, the computer operators take over. Computer operators are responsible for the running of jobs on the computer in accordance with operating instructions provided with the job by the programmer and systems analyst. These instructions will specify such details as what magnetic tape files are to be used, in what way certain errors will be indicated if they occur, and the action to be taken by the operator. One of the operators will have to be given responsibility for the library, unless the volume of work warrants the appointment of a full-time librarian. The library consists of the collection of files and programs held on magnetic tape or some other medium; to ensure the security of all information held in this way, someone must be given responsibility for controlling the issue and receipt of files and programs. In a small installation this responsibility may be given to one operator on each shift. The number of shifts worked will depend on the amount of work to be done; very late and very early shifts may cause some staff problems, but the tendency nowadays is increasingly to work multiple shifts in order to obtain a maximum return on the high capital cost of the equipment.

Data preparation staff and computer operators are usually grouped together in rooms located in close proximity, and the section is referred to as the DP unit. In a small installation the DP manager may be directly responsible for control of the DP unit; in a medium or large size department it is necessary to have someone called the operations manager, who is skilled at organizing and who has a knowledge of data processing, to control the DP unit. The success of any DP department depends ultimately on the efficiency of the DP unit, so that good organization and close control in this section are vital. Tight schedules have to be maintained, and documentation on the efficiency of programs and equipment and the progress of jobs through the DP unit, has constantly to be updated. The size and complexity of this task should not be underestimated.

Education for Data Processing

Education for data processing has two aspects; the training of staff who are in the DP department, and the enlightenment of other personnel as to the capabilities and limitations of a computer, and in what ways it will affect them in their work. Both of these aspects are extremely important since they will both have a decisive effect on the efficiency of the new computer system.

If insufficient training is given to DP staff, it should be self-evident that the new computer system stands little chance of success. All DP work demands skill and knowledge since the running of a computer system and, even more so, its installation, are complex operations. A generous time allowance should therefore be made in the installation schedule to permit adequate training of all DP staff. Most computer manufacturers provide a variety of short full-time courses of one or more weeks duration for the training of customers' staff. This initial training period should be supplemented by on-the-job training of new recruits by the more experienced members of the department. Data processing is a field subject to constant change so that training is best regarded as a continuing process. Opportunities to attend courses for extra training should always be open to DP staff, to improve their morale, and their value and commitment to the company. The demand for experienced DP staff currently exceeds the supply, so that they move frequently from company to company; opportunities to gain extra training can prove an attractive alternative to pay increases as an incentive to stay with one company.

Equally as important as the training of DP staff is the education of other staff who may be affected in their work by the installation of the computer. Recent research into the reasons why some new computer departments have not met their expected targets or produced the benefits forecast, has shown that a principal factor was the attitude of personnel outside the DP department. It is therefore imperative that the co-operation of these personnel be obtained. This can generally be achieved by encouraging executive management to participate actively in pre-installation proceedings, by chairing meetings of steering or working committees, and being present at talks for operatives. Executive management should also be advised of the policy-making implications of using a computer. Line managers must always attend meetings at which procedures for the new computer system that will affect their departments are discussed. In this way they can have a say in the form that the new procedures will take, and can then explain these to the staff of their department. Most computer manufacturers provide literature and films for the use of companies installing computers, and these can prove very effective in gaining the interest and involvement of staff.

The systems analyst will be particularly concerned with "selling" the new computer system. If he is to discover all the details of how a department's work is performed, of the unofficial system (the one by which work is *really* done, not the one by which it is supposed to be done), then he must first gain the confidence of the staff in the department in which he is currently working. Having gained their confidence in himself as a person, he must then get staff to accept the value of his job before he will persuade them to become involved with the new computer system. "Selling" a new computer system is not absolutely necessary, it can be imposed from above; but in this case it will work efficiently only for as long as it is maintained by those who have imposed it. The advantage of selling the new system is that it should prove to a large extent self-adaptive. That is to say, when difficulties occur, staff operating the system will themselves point out the problems and take steps to get them remedied, rather than wait for the DP staff to discover that something is going wrong, and leave them to find out what it is. This self-adaptive system can be obtained only if staff feel themselves involved in the system. An indication as to whether this goal is being achieved is the amount of feedback being obtained about the unofficial system. All companies have an unofficial system operating to some extent. Memos are for stating what everyone knows; the important information travels along the unofficial grapevine, and it is the job of the systems analyst to tap it. When he is on-line to the grapevine then there is a good chance that the new system is being accepted and that the involvement of staff can be obtained.

Site Preparation

Another very important item in the pre-installation schedule is the preparation of a site to house the computer and associated materials and staff. The work will progress from defining the site requirements to choosing a site and selecting contractors to undertake the construction work. An important factor is the need for an air-conditioned environment for the computer and magnetic storage media. The magnetic storage media, it is true, can be stored in hermetically sealed containers, and in this case need not be within the air-conditioned area. Extremes of temperature and humidity must, however, be avoided, and it is usually more practical to keep magnetic storage media in the same environment as the computer. The library will therefore usually be subject to the same environmental conditions as the computer, and so, too, will the engineer's room, provided for the use of the machine manufacturer's engineers who will maintain the equipment. Punched cards should be placed in the air-conditioned area for sufficient time to allow them to become acclimatized before they are used, and provision may be made for one to two days' supply to be stored in the library or computer room.

The amount of construction work involved in installing air-conditioning will depend on whether old buildings are being adapted or new ones erected. In the former case the air-conditioning engineers may be made the main contractors, with subcontractors to perform other tasks, whereas in the latter case the builder would probably be the main contractor. It is always preferable to engage contractors who have had experience of the same or a similar sort of work. All details of the tolerance limits of equipment as regards temperature and humidity, and advice on how to approach any problems that may arise, can be obtained from the machine manufacturer's engineers.

Apart from housing for the equipment, offices will have to be found for the staff of the DP department. It is generally preferable to have the whole department accommodated near the computer, although this is not strictly necessary except in the case of data preparation staff. Considerable thought should be given to the layout of the area surrounding the computer room so that the various rooms are arranged to reflect as nearly as possible the flow of work. An example of a layout for the operating area is given in Fig. 7.

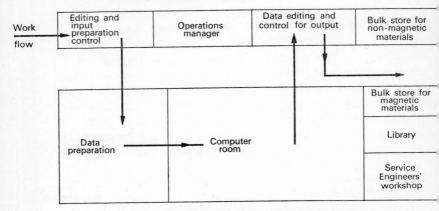

FIG. 7. Example of an operating area site layout.

File Conversion

File conversion is the transference of files of information from one medium to another, and may also involve some reorganization of the form in which files are held. Most of the difficulties which occur during this operation derive from the large volume of data that is usually involved and from the fact that the normal daily work load must be carried out at the same time. Problems may also arise from the inexperience of DP staff when file conversion is started, and other departments may display initial concern since the commencement of file conversion is likely to be the first time that they are affected in their work by the installation of the new computer system.

File conversion may simply involve transferring punched-card files on to magnetic tape by means of a conversion program. More usually, however, particularly where existing files are maintained manually, it is necessary to reorganize files. Data has to be collected and assembled from many different sources, validated, recorded on special punching documents, and punched, before it can be transferred to magnetic tape. In general, several months are needed to complete file conversion, and this time is preceded by weeks of planning.

When the new system is designed, the systems analyst will include in the systems definition details of the procedures to be followed for file conversion. Supplementary planning will invariably be needed, however, and this cannot be started too early. The time at which file conversion must be started depends on the estimate of how long it will take. The volume of the files to be converted, the time needed to gather and prepare data and to punch cards, and whether the punching is to be done by employing extra staff, working overtime, or by sending work to an outside agency, are all factors to be taken into account. In the first two cases allowance must be made for training staff to use punches. Yet another consideration is whether files are to be converted piecemeal over a period of time, or whether the new system is to become operative on one particular date. A less tangible factor is the degree to which acceptance of the new system being installed has been gained, and the importance of file conversion realized in the departments affected. If conversion is given a low priority, and fitted in only at odd convenient moments when other work is slack, then this will obviously be a serious delaying factor. Delay of this sort can be avoided if a schedule for conversion is drawn up and departmental managers encouraged to adhere to it.

Data for conversion is usually divided into two categories—static and variable. Static data is that which is subject only to infrequent changes, such as customers' names and addresses; variable data includes such items as transactions and balances, which are constantly changing. Static data can be assembled and punched earlier than variable data, since it will require comparatively little updating. Thus static data may be transferred to magnetic tape at any convenient time near to the changeover date, and merged with variable data when the changeover to the new computer system is effected.

There are basically three different procedures for effecting the changeover—direct changeover, parallel operation, and pilot operation. The direct changeover is a very dangerous procedure, and to be recommended only when there is no feasible alternative. If, for instance, there is no similarity between the inputs and outputs of the old and new systems, a direct changeover may be the only worth-while procedure. This procedure is also sometimes employed where the volume of work involved in parallel operation renders this alternative impractical. In such cases, however, a staggered implementation of the new system by pilot operation may prove a better choice.

Parallel operation involves running both old and new systems concurrently, cross-checking the outputs from both systems to verify that the new system is working satisfactorily. This procedure is usually operated for one complete processing cycle, the outputs of the old system being used for distribution. This is perhaps the safest method of introducing a new system, but involves a great deal of extra work; the old system should therefore be discontinued as soon as possible.

One form of pilot operation involves processing data from a previous period on the new system. The results of the processing are already known, and thus the efficiency of the new system can be checked. This procedure has the advantage of being susceptible to greater control by the systems analysts and line supervisors, since the incoming data and correct results are already known. The second form of pilot operation involves introducing the new system in piecemeal fashion. This procedure can best be adopted where the work breaks down easily into logical units; one unit at a time is converted to the new system, while the old system continues to function for the remaining units. As more work is converted to be run on the new system, the old system is gradually discontinued. A frequent compromise is to adopt this last procedure but to run each unit of work in parallel operation for a short time after it is converted. In this way the advantages of implementing a new system gradually, with the consequent easing of pressure on file conversion time, are combined with the extra safety factor inherent in parallel operation.

Whatever changeover procedure is adopted, it should essentially suit the organization and the old and new system concerned. The ultimate objective should be to ensure the reliability of the new system and to bring it into operation as smoothly as is possible.

Control

The introduction of electronic equipment into data processing has considerably altered methods of controlling the accuracy and validity of information. It is no longer feasible to check individual transactions as they are being processed; the increasing tendency to integrate the various functions of an organization has resulted in the loss of many of the visible records previously kept for checking purposes, and in difficulty in finding defined trails through all the data. Computer processing, moreover, has not the advantage, gained by manual processing, of permitting checks by human initiative every time each item is processed.

However, if human initiative provides a means of control, it is also a serious source of errors; electronic machines, although lacking in initiative, are not subject to human errors, and thus need relatively little control when working independently. It is at times of human intervention and when mechanical equipment is being used that errors are most likely to occur, and so it is on these points that control needs to be concentrated; that is to say, on the validation of input data and the verification of output data.

Clearly it is always advantageous to eliminate errors at their source; however, it is even better to eliminate the source of error itself. While it is not possible to eliminate intervention by people or the use of mechanical devices, it is possible to eliminate such sources of error as bad organization and anarchy in the realm of procedures and documentation. It is vitally important that the organizational structure of a company should be clearly defined, and that personnel should fully comprehend the duties and responsibilities attached to their jobs. Any laxity in this respect will result in personnel either assuming conflicting responsibilities or no responsibility at all, with disastrous results in either case. Another important factor in the degree of control attained will be the extent to which staff have accepted and become involved with the new computer system. The involvement of staff is critical, since one effect of the introduction of a computer will be to increase the number of clerical grade staff performing preparation, editing, verification, and control functions. If this work is carried out assiduously, as it will be if staff identify themselves with their work, then work should flow smoothly through the DP unit. If this work is not well done, it will result in errors going through to the machine; if errors are detected at that stage, the data will be rejected and have to be reprocessed, with possibly a consequent wastage of very expensive machine time.

An added emphasis on control is the principal effect that computers have had on the work of the auditor. He now seeks less to ascertain the accuracy of data than to satisfy himself that controls are entirely adequate to ensure that data is accurate. Provided that the auditor is consulted when controls are being decided upon, his co-operation should be assured.

CHAPTER 4

Information from Data Processing

Why Process Data?

It is the purpose of this chapter to explain the way in which data is organized in a computer system in contrast to a manual system, and to give the reader an appreciation of the superior quality of information, in terms of speed, accuracy, and relevance, that can be obtained by using a computer. All this demands an understanding of the fundamental reasons why data is processed and stored.

One good reason for processing data is that the customer requires it. When the goods which he has ordered are delivered, he wishes to see exactly what he has been charged for and how much. This implies the need for an invoicing system. Similarly, employees want to know why there is less money in their pay packet than they feel they are entitled to, and how the deductions from gross salary are accounted for. It is therefore necessary to prepare pay advice slips. This sort of data, although necessary in order to satisfy customer, personnel, or legal requirements, may be the least important as far as the company is concerned, since the company may derive no material benefit from it. It does not serve to control any process, neither does it provide any profitable information. It need not, however, cause any great inconvenience or extra work if it can be produced by a by-product of processing data which is essential to the running of the company.

The principal reasons for data processing are to control the current work of a company and to plan and schedule future work. There is an interaction between data produced for these two reasons, since information regarding current work is used in summarized form to assess work done, and as historical data to provide a basis for future plans and schedules. The sales force might start a cycle of data flow by submitting a batch of orders collected in the field. These orders might be satisfied from existing stocks, or the goods requested might have to be manufactured; in either case, invoices will have to be prepared. If the goods are to be supplied from existing stocks, stores have to be notified of the order, and the items supplied deleted from the inventory; if this results in existing stocks falling below a certain level, production have to be notified that new stock is required. Production in turn have to notify the section which keeps supplies of primary materials, and if the stock of these is insufficient, new supplies have to be ordered. As primary materials go to production, through the various production units, until the manufactured goods arrive to build up stocks for sale, so there will be a corresponding flow of data to account for the materials used and the man hours spent, and to indicate the progress of work at any given time. It can thus be seen that large amounts of data are produced merely owing to the need to control the current work of the company. However, apart from the function of immediate control, this data has another very important use.

Individually, the items of data produced as shown above have no long-term relevance. Summarized, however, these items provide a complete picture of the company's work. It is impossible for a company to plan its future work properly if it has no clear idea of how current work is progressing; the summarized data is used to provide the necessary information. Over a period of time the summarized data, analysed by valid statistical techniques, provides information as to the nature, amount, and frequency of orders, whether these are satisfied from existing stocks or involve waiting for production, and the average time taken to supply given types of order. Such analysis can indicate where any deficiencies in the company's systems are to be found, and provide a basis for assessing the performance of various divisions of the company. Further analysis using operational research techniques, and allied to some market research, can indicate what plans the company should make for the future and how it can improve its efficiency generally and thus increase its profit margin. As a result of this analysis of summarized historical data, senior management can make policy decisions on the basis of scientifically assessed recent information, rather than on the basis of intuition and hazily formulated principles culled from experience gained from days long past and often completely irrelevant to current situations. Moreover, once policy decisions are put into practice, the continuing flow of data which complements the company's work is analysed as usual to allow an accurate assessment of the effect of the last policy decisions, and an indication as to what the next ones should be. Such information permits a company to adapt as rapidly as possible to the changing conditions of the commercial environment in which it exists.

File Organization

It is a curious fact that while DP experts in general consider all "paperwork" as inherently bad and best eliminated wherever possible, the usual result of installing a computer system is to increase the amount of data flowing around a company. This apparent paradox has a very reasonable explanation, as will be seen. The fundamental problem of data processing may be stated as follows. If a company is to be run successfully, senior management must make the right policy decisions; in order to make the right decisions, senior management must have all the relevant facts to hand, and this involves analysing large amounts of data. Collecting and analysing large amounts of data takes time, and the longer the time taken the less up to date, and hence less relevant, the information obtained. In short, the benefit gained through taking more factors into account is nullified by the time that this takes.

In a manual system there is virtually no way round this problem. It is the usual practice, where files are maintained manually, to duplicate information in order to reduce the time necessary to access individual items of data held within files. To take a simplified example, suppose that details of all sales are held on files, and that since the sales force is organized on an area basis the files are too. Comprehensive details of all sales will be contained in the sales reports which are submitted at regular intervals, and are duly filed away for reference in sales area sequence and chronological order. Information on any specific sale can then be readily accessed. Suppose, however, that information is required on all sales by a certain salesman, or to a certain customer, or type of customer, or of a specific product? Such information could be obtained only by hunting through the whole of the sales report file, and this would have to be done every time the information was required. In order to avoid such a long procedure, relevant information in the sales reports is duplicated, and several files are set up. Thus, basically the same information would appear in several files, one of which would be indexed by the names of salesmen, another by the type of product, another by the type of customer, and so on. This necessitates a large amount of storage space, and means that each sales report received involves updating not one, but several files. If at any time, additional information is required, it is necessary either to create a new file and hence increase storage space, or to accept long delays in accessing items of data from current files. This dilemma is inherent in the use of manually maintained files.

It can be seen that what is needed is a means of accessing individual items quickly from among large volumes of data; this is exactly what the computer provides, and not only this, but also the facility to keep much larger records than would be practical in any manual system. Since the time needed to access any item of data held, for instance, in an exchangeable disc store, is very short, the number of items of which a record is composed has only a small significance. The time taken by a filing clerk to search through a hundred items of data on a record rather than five items, is out of all proportion to the corresponding time taken by a computer. Thus, whereas the tendency in manual filing systems is to create new files, when a changeover to a computer system is made, separate manual files are integrated to form complex computer files. Moreover, since access times are low, a great deal of extra useful information can be included on records. It may have been realized that the availability of some extra information would be of use to managers, but fear of swamping the manual filing system may have prevented this information being retained. The change to a computer system provides an opportunity for such information to be included in files without significantly increasing access time, and without causing the system to collapse under the strain. Hence the apparent paradox mentioned above. Thus, taking the example of sales files once again, if the sales reports contained a large amount of narrative or essential diagrams, these would be filed manually as before, and used as a library for cases where whole reports were required. All important items of data in the reports would be duplicated on to one computer file, which would be used to answer all queries whether these were related to salesmen, producers, or customers. It would be possible, but expensive, to answer all queries immediately; the usual practice is to run batches of queries against the master file at intervals appropriate to the general urgency of requests for information.

Performance Standards

It has been stated above that summarized data can be used as a basis for producing plans and schedules for the future. An important concept in this process is the formulation of performance standards. Planning necessarily involves some form of scheduling, and scheduling is not possible unless the work rate of personnel and machines is known. There is therefore a need for some method of gauging the quality and quantity of work performed, and this is the function of performance standards. Performance standards, if drawn up realistically on the basis of past performance, provide a yardstick against which current work can be measured. Management has no means of assessing the value of work actually performed if there is no yardstick against which it can be measured. It is essential, therefore, that management should know how much work *ought* to be done in a certain time in order to assess whether that actually completed is sufficient. The ability to measure both the quality and quantity of work is a constant management need, not only to assess the value of work performed but also in order to be able to develop realistic schedules and budgets. The time needed to perform a task cannot be accurately estimated unless the rate of working of the personnel involved is known; upon the time taken will also depend the cost to perform the task. Neither time schedule nor budget can accurately be estimated without some form of performance standards. Performance standards also provide a means of assessing personnel with a view to their promotion and a way of evaluating new experienced staff and the potential of inexperienced staff. In short, performance standards are essential to control and planning, two principal functions of the manager; they are both derived from, and provide a means of evaluating, the information received by a manager.

Scientific Management

The revolution that is taking place in modern data processing has greatly facilitated the replacement of intuition and experience by scientific method as an approach to modern business problems. Although intuition and experience have still a part to play, it is self-evident that those processes in commerce and industry which are rational, and most processes are, can best be treated in a rational manner. Such treatment demands complete and accurate information, however, and the collection, retention, and manipulation, of the large volumes of data involved has not until recent years been feasible. It is in this respect that the revolutionary effects of the computer have been seen. Projects are now undertaken which only a few years ago were deemed impossible, not because the necessary knowledge was not available, but because the sheer effort involved would have taken a large number of men an inordinately long time. Projects do not have to be large, however, to realize benefits from the user of a computer. Individual commercial processes can be understood in greater detail, work more closely controlled, and more speedily adapted to a changing environment than has ever before been possible.

PLATE I. Card machine used in the 1890 census.
(*Courtesy of the Science Museum*)

PLATE II. Console typewriter.

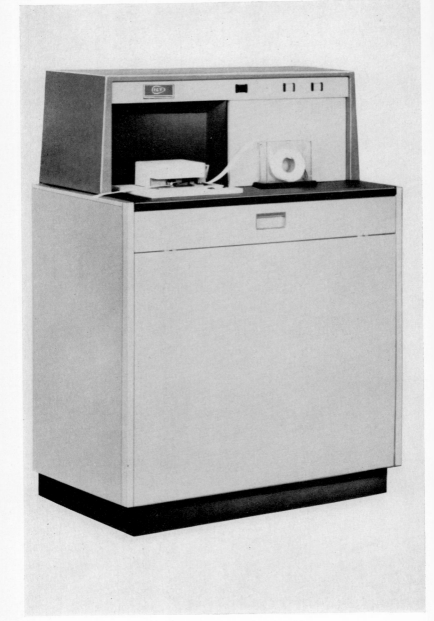

PLATE III. Paper tape reader.

PLATE IV. Magnetic tape units.

PLATE V. Line printer.

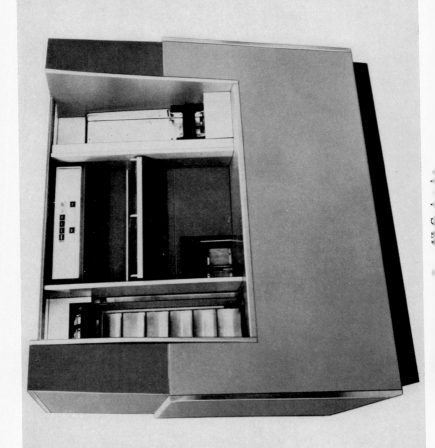

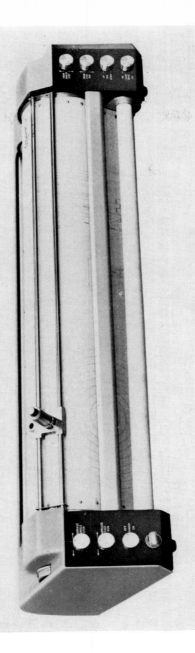

PLATE VII. Graph plotter.

PLATE VIII. Visual display unit.

PLATE IX. Exchangeable disc store.

PLATE X. Central processor.

PART II

Scientific Management

some concepts
and techniques which
should be understood
are first expl
before application
to specific a

CHAPTER 5

Scientific Management Techniques

THE use of a computer alone will not analyse and provide possible solutions to the complex problems associated with modern business. A company must first realize what its problems are, and devise methods of solving them, before a computer can be programmed to implement the methods of extracting and analysing information which have been devised. In many cases such research into business problems will require a high degree of mathematical ability, and is thus the province of operational research specialists. Few managers can be expected to spend time considering the details of mathematical formulae devised and used by these specialists; this should not deter managers, however, from gaining an understanding of the principles on which operational research is based. Scientific management is essentially a state of mind, requiring a rational approach to business problems and not a first-class honours degree in mathematics. It is the purpose of the succeeding chapters to show, without recourse to advanced mathematics, how marketing problems can be approached rationally and dealt with methodically, and particularly how a computer can prove an invaluable tool to management. Some concepts and techniques which should be understood are first explained before their application to specific areas of work and problems in the marketing field are described.

Statistical Analysis

The term statistical analysis covers a large number of techniques for obtaining significant information from volumes of data which

54   *Marketing and the Computer*

have no readily apparent meaning. The data that is available through the normal work processes of a company is rarely in a form from which accurate conclusions can be drawn. Moreover it is often dangerous to guess at the implications of a mass of "raw" data, since even if some trend is apparent, appearances may be misleading. Volumes of data are therefore collected and subjected to methodical analysis by proven techniques in order to obtain accurate and significant information. There are many examples of the usefulness of statistical techniques applied to business data.

Sampling is a method used to reduce the volume of data from which accurate conclusions can be drawn. Provided that a sample is representative of the total volume of data from which it has been selected, any inference drawn from the sample should be equally true of all the data. A sample, however, is much easier to manipulate or analyse in order to extract significance from it.

It is frequently difficult to assess trends in orders, particularly if the orders are subject to seasonal or some other variations. Given the order figures below (Table 5), it is not difficult to see that the general trend is upwards, but it is very difficult to see the extent

TABLE 5. ORDER FIGURES (PRODUCT X)

Year	1st quarter	2nd quarter	3rd quarter	4th quarter
1964	573	231	258	300
1965	625	263	290	324
1966	670	319	332	369

of the trend. By exponential smoothing of these figures, however, it is possible to assess the exact nature of the trend. It can be seen that orders for the first quarter are relatively high, and orders for the second quarter relatively low. This pattern repeats itself every four quarters, so that four quarters may be taken as an order cycle. By taking an average quarterly figure from the total orders for a cycle, the seasonal variation can be smoothed out. This is illustrated in Table 6. However, the average figure taken in this way applies to a point in time midway between the second and third quarters of the cycle. In order to obtain an average figure which applies to the end of each quarter, it is necessary to take the average of pairs of successive cycle figures. Thus, in Table 6 column 1 contains the order figures for each quarter; column 2

TABLE 6. EXPONENTIAL SMOOTHING OF ORDERS FIGURES

Year	Quarter	Quarterly orders figures 1	Sum of quarters 1–4, 2–5, etc. (cycles) 2	Sum of cycles 1+2, 2+3, etc. 3	Sum of cycles ÷ 8 giving smoothed quarterly figures 4
1	1	573			
	2	231			
			1362		
	3	258		2776	347
			1414		
	4	300		2860	357
			1446		
2	1	625		2924	365
			1478		
	2	263		2980	372
			1502		
	3	290		3049	381
			1547		
	4	324		3150	394
			1603		
3	1	670	1647	3250	406
				3339	
	2	319	1692		417
	3	332			
	4	369			

contains the sum of order figures for four successive quarters, constituting an order cycle, e.g. the sum of quarters 1–4, 2–5, 3–6, and so on. Column 3 contains the sum of pairs of successive cycle figures, and column 4 the smoothed average order figure for each quarter, obtained by dividing column 3 by 8. It can be seen that the figures in column 4 show a much clearer trend than those in column 1. This is illustrated even more clearly in the accompanying graph (Fig. 8).

A company needs not only to know how to assess its past and current performance, but also to estimate what is likely to happen

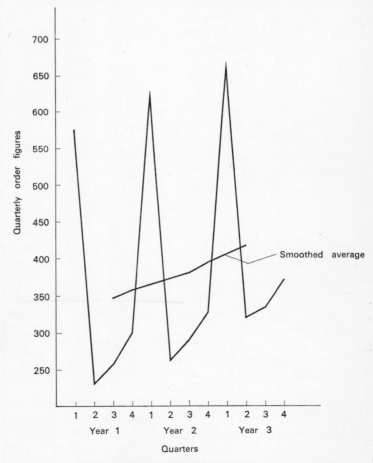

FIG. 8. Graph of exponential smoothing.

in the future. It may, for instance, want to know the amount and type of orders it is likely to receive in the year ahead. The general trend in orders has already been established; a more detailed examination of the orders figures could show the size of individual orders, the frequency with which orders of a given size occurred, the category of customer submitting given orders, and other such useful information. By means of the statistical theory of probability, it would then be possible to estimate the likelihood of orders of a certain type and amount occurring at a given time. This information could be invaluable in assessing the level of stocks which should be held ready for sale at any time.

Obviously, many factors can affect the type and amount of orders received; advertising, the size and quality of the sales force, the number of competitors in the field, whether orders can be met directly from stock, and numerous other factors play their part. Most commercial processes are similarly influenced by a number of related factors; what management needs to know is the nature of the relationship between the various factors, or variables as they are called. By further statistical analyses of historical data, it is often possible to establish a coefficient of correlation between the variables affecting a given process, and once this has been done, to estimate the effect that changing the value of one variable will have on other variables and the whole process.

Elementary statistical techniques such as sampling, exponential smoothing, calculation of the coefficient of correlation, regression analysis, and the theory of probability form the basis of more advanced techniques which are an essential aid to modern management. While a manager need not be familiar with statistical intricacies, he should appreciate the principles and uses of these techniques. All those mentioned above will be further explained and illustrated in the succeeding pages.

Linear Programming

Linear programming is one of the most fundamental of scientific management techniques and is sometimes described as the "bread and butter" of operational research. The importance of linear programming derives from the large number of problems in industry and commerce to which the technique can be applied, although there are certain restrictions on its use. The term "programming" implies the use of computers, and although large jobs can usually be processed economically only on a computer, small jobs may be adequately processed manually. The term "linear" is used because the quantities involved in a problem to which this technique is to be applied must have a linear relationship. For example, a relationship between three quantities, A, B, and C such that $A = 2B + 3C$ would be valid, whereas the relationship $A = B^2 + C^2$ would not, since in the latter case the relationship between A and the other quantities is quadratic and not linear. This restriction on the use of linear programming does not seriously limit its importance to commerce, since a large number of factors in commerce have linear relationships. The cost of raw materials, for instance, rises in proportion to the amount ordered; the amount ordered rises in proportion to the quantity of products being manufactured; the cost of stock keeping rises with the amount of stock held, and so on. Another prerequisite for linear programming is that all the factors associated with a problem must have a numerical value. The values of each factor, unit cost for instance, must therefore be known.

Associated with the variables concerned in the problem will usually be one or more constraints. There may be a limit on the amount of space available to hold stock, or on the quantities of raw materials available, or there may be a limit on the amount of money available for specific purposes. Given such constraints, and known numerical values for each of the variables, linear programming is used to optimize usually just one of the variables. The optimization may be to produce either a maximum or a minimum; for instance, maximum profit or minimum cost. The choice as to which variable is to be optimized is a management decision. The usual criterion which will be adopted is that of maximum profit, but circumstances may sometimes cause other criteria to be given a higher priority. A lack of available cash might, for instance, mean that it was imperative to reduce costs even if this caused profits to be curtailed in the short term.

The general approach to a problem by linear programming is to consider the constraints first of all; in this way the area in which a feasible solution may be found is limited. In order to illustrate this technique, a simple example is given below involving two variables and three constraints. It is desired to determine the proportion of two products that should be made in order to yield the maximum profit. The two products, X_1 and X_2, are made from three raw materials, R_1, R_2, and R_3. One ton of X_1 requires 2 tons of R_1 and 1 ton of R_2, and yields a profit of £10. One ton of X_2 requires 1 ton of each of R_1, R_2, and R_3 and yields a profit of £20. There is a limit on the resources that may be used, since only 300 tons of R_1, 200 tons of R_2, and 150 tons of R_3 are available. Since only two variables, X_1 and X_2 are involved, this example can be illustrated graphically. Given the proportions of each raw material that go into the manufacture of X_1 and X_2, and the maximum amount of each raw material available, the following constraints apply:

$$\text{For } R_1: \quad 2X_1 + X_2 \leqslant 300 \text{ tons}$$
$$\text{For } R_2: \quad X_1 + X_2 \leqslant 200 \text{ tons}$$
$$\text{For } R_3: \qquad\quad X_2 \leqslant 150 \text{ tons}$$

The graph is constructed with each of the axes representing one of the variables. The above constraints are drawn in so that the line R_1, for instance, represents any production programme which uses up to the 300 tons available. Any point on this line, or to the left of it, represents a feasible solution as far as the availability of resources is concerned. Similarly with lines R_1 and R_3, so that a feasible solution must lie within the area bounded by the X_1 and X_2 axes, and the lines R_1, R_2, and R_3. The solution thus far is illustrated in Fig. 9, where the area of feasible solution is shaded in.

It has already been stated that 1 ton of X_1 yields £10 profit, and 1 ton of X_2 £20 profit. The profit to be maximized is therefore $10X_1 + 20X_2$, which is represented on the graph by any line cutting the X_1 and X_2 axes such that $X_1 = 2X_2$. A line parallel to any such line, but passing through the point zero, represents no profit. As this line is moved up, so the profit increases. This is illustrated in Fig. 10. As can be seen, either 50 tons of X_2 or 100 tons of X_1 will yield £1000 profit. Any combination of X_1 and X_2 represented by a point on this line will also yield £1000 profit.

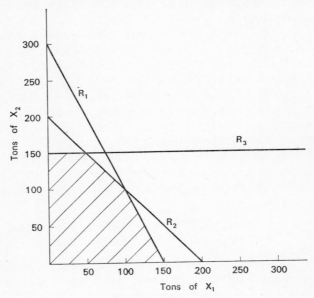

FIG. 9. The constraints.

The further the profit line from the datum (zero), the higher the profit. The line, however, is limited by the resource availability constraints previously described, so that it can now be seen that maximum profit is to be obtained by finding the furthest point from the profit datum line which is still within the resource constraint line. This point is easily recognized if the two graphs illustrated above are combined as in Fig. 11. The solution for maximum profit is therefore to produce 50 tons of X_1 and 150 tons of X_2, yielding £500 + £3000 = £3500 profit.

The example that has been described is very simple, but has the advantage of showing the principles of linear programming, and since it involves only two variables, graphical illustration is possible. The inclusion of a third variable product X_3, would require a further axis at right angles to the X_1 and X_2 axes. The profit and constraint lines would then become planes, and the

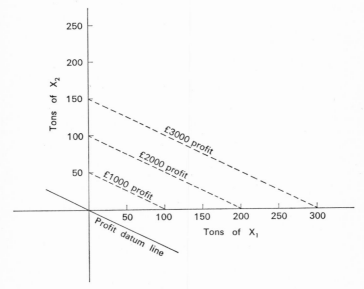

FIG. 10. The profit line.

resultant figure would have to be left to the reader's imagination. In practice, a large number of constraints and variables will usually be involved, resulting in highly complex structures. The calculations associated with these complex structures can be lengthy and repetitious, requiring weeks of manual effort or a matter of seconds of computer time.

Linear programming is most frequently used to solve problems of distribution, blending, and transportation. Certain refinements of the general technique have been devised to suit specific problems, as for instance, the transportation technique. Formulating purchasing policy, determining the optimum size of a bid, and rationing scarce products to the best markets, are all problems to which linear programming has been applied. Further illustrations of the use of this technique will be given later in this book.

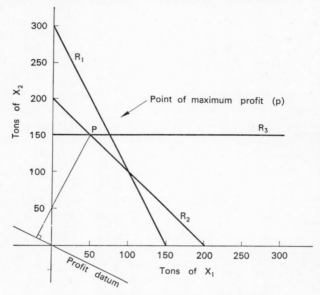

FIG. 11. The solution for maximum profit.

Queueing Theory

Queueing theory, as the term suggests, is the study of queues and their behaviour. The word queue is used with the same meaning as in a queue of people at a bus stop. Although this example may have small relevance to commerce, a little thought should reveal a number of situations in commerce in which similar conditions apply. An order book, for instance, may be considered as a queue of customers waiting to be served; an inventory may be considered as a queue of goods either to be used in production or to be sold. In all these situations items join the queue while others leave. The object of queueing theory is to establish the probable size of a queue at any given time, and in this way to determine ways of controlling the queue so that it may be kept at a certain size or perhaps completely eliminated.

The theory of probability and the generation of random numbers are closely concerned with queueing theory. In some cases items will either join or leave queues at fixed intervals; stocks, for instance, may be replenished at fixed intervals, or products may leave a production line at fixed intervals. More frequently, however, items will join or leave queues at random intervals. Orders may be received in any quantity at any time, and demands on stocks of spare parts cannot be precisely forecast. Moreover, as control of many commercial processes becomes tighter and more precise, there is a tendency to discard such practices as ordering fixed quantities of stock, or ordering at fixed intervals, in order to have greater flexibility to take advantage of the precise control that can now be achieved. Where additions to and reductions from a queue occur randomly, it is necessary to estimate the probability of items either leaving or joining the queue. By observation of current processes, or analysis of historical data, it is possible to establish at what rate the queue changes in size. Given an average number of changes to the queue occurring in a specified time interval, it is possible to estimate the probability of any number of changes occurring in that same time. Management can then decide what range of probabilities is to be allowed for, and thus what servicing the queue will require.

The following simplified problem will give an illustration of the basic principles of queueing theory. Suppose that a manufacturer has found that there have been excessive delays in satisfying requests for spare parts from stock, and that it is desired to establish a new level of stock that will reduce or eliminate delays without, however, keeping an excessive surplus stock. For the purposes of this example it will be assumed that stock is reviewed at weekly intervals, and that the numbers of each spare part placed in stock weekly must be fixed. The demand for all spare parts would need to be examined, but only the case of spare part X will be examined here.

Records of the requests for spare part X over the preceding 26 weeks are collected and the weekly demand for this part examined. The figures given in column 1 of Table 7 are produced, showing that the demand varies from three to seventeen parts per week. Moreover, it can be seen that the demand from one week to the next varies greatly, so that the number of parts requested one

TABLE 7. SPARE PART FIGURES

Weekly demand	Order level 9 parts per week	Requests waiting 1 week	Requests waiting 2 weeks	Order level 10 parts per week	Requests waiting 1 day
1	2	3	4	5	6
17	−8	8		−7	7
7	−6	6		−4	4
9	−6	6		−3	3
17	−14	9	5	−10	10
7	−12	4	3	−7	7
4	−7	4		−1	1
4	−2	2		+5	
4	+3			+11	
5	+7			+16	
7	+9			+19	
14	+4			+15	
8	+5			+17	
11	+3			+16	
13	−1	1		+13	
8	0			+15	
7	+2			+18	
4	+7			+24	
13	+3			+21	
14	−2	2		+17	
14	−7	7		+13	
9	−7	7		+14	
16	−14	9	5	+8	
13	−18	4	9	+5	
3	−12		3	+12	
9	−12	6	3	+13	
13	−16	6	7	+10	

week is no guide to the number that is likely to be requested during the following week. A short calculation will show that the average number of spare part X requested per week is 9.6. It follows from this that a reasonable level of stock ordering would be either 9 or 10 parts per week. The consequences that would have followed from restocking with 9 parts per week during this period are shown in column 2. Minus values indicate the number of requests for part X waiting to be satisfied, and positive values indicate the number of spare parts held over in stock from one week to the next. It can be seen from these figures that the number of parts held in excess of weekly demand is never very high; in fact never as much as one week's average demand. On the other hand, for over half the number of weeks requests for spare part X have to be kept waiting until succeeding weeks in order to be satisfied. An analysis of the figures in column 2 is given in columns 3 and 4 showing the number of requests having to wait 1 and 2 weeks respectively. In order to calculate queueing time in weeks, the number of requests having to wait is multiplied by the number of weeks each waits, and the total divided by the total number of requests received. This gives an average queueing time for a request of 0.6 of a week

$$
\begin{aligned}
81 \text{ spare parts} \times 1 \text{ week} &= 81 \\
35 \text{ spare parts} \times 2 \text{ weeks} &= 70 \\
\text{Total} &\quad 151 \\
\text{Total number of requests} &= 250
\end{aligned}
$$

$151 \div 250 = 0.6$ weeks (approx.) average queueing time

Thus the average queueing time does not seem excessive, although its actual importance can be judged only by the company concerned. Moreover, it has been assumed that a request not satisfied one week would have to wait at least one whole week, and this is not necessarily true. A request received towards the end of one week might be satisfied at the beginning of the next. Assuming that the requests are evenly distributed throughout the week, the probability is that an unsatisfied request would have to wait on average only one half of a week. Besides which, if requests are dealt with chronologically, it is the requests received towards the end of a week that are more likely to have to wait. Thus, repeating the above calculation, but substituting a half and $1\frac{1}{2}$ weeks for 1 and 2 weeks respectively, a new average queueing time is produced.

$$
\begin{array}{ll}
81 \text{ spare parts} \times \tfrac{1}{2} \text{ week} & = 40.5 \\
35 \text{ spare parts} \times 1\tfrac{1}{2} \text{ weeks} & = \underline{52.5} \\
\text{Total} & = 93 \\
\text{Total number of requests} & = 250
\end{array}
$$

$93 \div 250 = 0.4$ weeks (approx.) average queueing time

This reduced figure is obviously more acceptable than the previous one; even so, management may decide that the waiting time is still too long. The alternative in this case is to increase the weekly order level to 10 spare parts. The consequences that would have followed from this policy are shown in columns 5 and 6. Waiting for requests to be satisfied is virtually eliminated; on the other hand, the number of spare parts held in stock is at times in excess of 2 weeks' average demand. The actual average queueing time, derived as in the previous calculations, is approximately 0.1 of a week if one week is regarded as the shortest waiting time, and 0.06 of a week if one-half a week is regarded as the shortest waiting time. These results of the analysis of the problem would be placed before management; it would be up to management to decide which policy to pursue.

This illustration of an application of queueing theory is greatly simplified. Further illustrations of queueing theory will be given in the explanation of simulation and later in the book.

Simulation

The techniques described so far have all involved an analytical approach in their application to business problems, the object of the analysis being to isolate the factors affecting a situation and establish a mathematical relationship between them. In some cases, however, this form of approach is either impossible or impractical. There may be no known way of analysing a situation, or it may be that the number of factors affecting the situation is so large, and their interrelationships so complex, that to attempt to analyse them would be uneconomic, and the eventual result so complex as to render its use impractical even with the aid of a computer. In these cases, instead of the situation being analysed, it is observed, and from repeated observations a model is built up that in its significant aspects reacts in the same way as the original situation. Thus the situation being studied is simulated.

Simulation is a technique for obtaining information about a situation by constructing a model that behaves in the same way as the original situation in all essential details. It is most frequently applied to dynamic situations, those that change continuously with the passage of time. Such situations usually involve one or more queues whose length varies randomly. It has been stated earlier, for instance, that orders received from the field are random in their size and in the frequency with which they occur. Similarly, even the best regulated production line is subject to hazards which render its output variable. Both the order book and the production line are queues; more accurately, the production line consists of a number of related queues, since a queue may be formed at each stage in the production process as items pass from one stage of production to the next. Associated with each queue is a scheduling problem and an inventory problem; How many? How frequently? When? Moreover, when the production processes have finished, there is still the problem of delivery, and another one or more queues. When the situation to be studied involves a large number of related queues there is often only one answer: simulation.

Basically, simulation involves making lists of items at each stage in the situation under study at which a queue is formed, and transferring individual items from one queue to another in the correct chronological order. In this way the state of a queue, and of the whole process, can be observed at any given time. It would be possible to carry out this procedure manually, but this would be so laborious in all but the most simple cases that a computer becomes an essential aid in the use of the technique.

Since simulation is not an analytical technique, it is not used to discover a unique solution to a problem. Instead possible courses of action, or policies are devised by management and applied to the model which simulates the real situation. For each policy there will be a different reaction from the model, so that management is provided with not an optimum solution, but a choice of policy decisions whose results are known with the degree of accuracy that the model reflects the real situation. A great advantage of simulation can now be seen; using this technique, various policy decisions can be taken in theory, and their effects assessed, without the expense of putting them into practice on a trial-and-error basis being incurred. The most suitable policy can then be selected, and that one alone put into effect. Because of this facility for simulating the effects of decisions, management may think more freely, and consider policies that might be thought too dangerous if the only way of seeing their effects was to put them into practice.

The use of the technique of simulation can be illustrated with reference to the example given in the explanation of queueing theory. It will be remembered that in this example conclusions were drawn from a set of weekly order figures that covered a 6-month period. Although these figures might in fact be representative, it is unlikely that any policy decisions would be based on them in practice if there was the possibility that significant variations would occur. Supposing that the overall pattern of the figures is representative, it would at least be wise to formulate variations in individual figures within the general pattern before deciding that a particular inventory policy was suitable. Thus the general pattern of requests for spare part X might be taken as a distribution of figures in the range 0–20 with a mean of between 9 and 10; wider variations could be allowed for if this was thought necessary. A computer could then be programmed to generate random numbers conforming to this general pattern, and a model of the requests situation thereby constructed. If more details were required, a model of the daily situation could be constructed using the same principles. The alternative policies of restocking with either 9 or 10 spare parts per week could then be applied to this situation, and the effects of each policy assessed with more assurance.

Given an accurate model of the basic situation, however, management might be tempted to experiment with other inventory policies. The various possibilities of restocking with fixed quantities at variable intervals, variable quantities at fixed intervals, or having both variable quantities and intervals, with a range of values given to both the quantity and interval parameters, could all be applied to the basic situation of requests for spare part X. This would, of course, necessitate a large amount of calculation, but the amount of effort involved would be greatly reduced with the aid of a computer.

PERT

PERT stands for the Project Evaluation and Review Technique, a method of planning and progressing large or complex operations. This technique was originally devised for use in the POLARIS project, but has since found numerous other applications. Other similar techniques have been devised and developed in parallel with PERT, and have given rise to other names such as critical path analysis, critical path method, critical path planning, and so on. The principles on which all these techniques are based are the same, however, and these are explained below. The PERT technique is frequently used in the installation of a computer, and since this is an example suitable to this book, the ensuing explanation will be given with this application in mind.

PERT is a form of network analysis. Any project can be broken down into stages or activities which are interrelated in some way, and the relationships expressed diagramatically in the form of lines and nodes which together make up a network. In this network, which appears rather like a map of roads linking towns, a line represents an activity and a node an event. This is illustrated in Fig. 12.

An activity, as the term is used in association with the PERT technique, may be defined as any operation which requires time and/or resources. Although activities are represented by lines, the length of a line bears no relation to the time or resources involved in the activity; lines indicate merely that an activity exists, and help define its relationship with other activities. The size of activities may vary considerably, the object being to break down the overall project into units of manageable size. Therefore it could be said that an activity should be the smallest unit over which management wishes to exercise control. Occasionally it may be necessary to include dummy activities in a network, these being

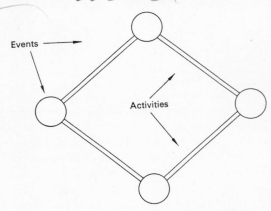

FIG. 12. Events and activities.

used to indicate a relationship between two events, but not requiring any time or resources. Sometimes an activity may start during a preceding activity, and be progressively fed by the first activity so that there is a lead time prior to the start of the second activity and a lag time after the end of the first activity. Such occurrences are represented on the network in the form of a ladder, where the lead and lag times are represented by the sides of the ladder. Both dummy and ladder activities are shown in Fig. 13.

A node on the network represents an event which may be defined in this context as a point in time which may be the

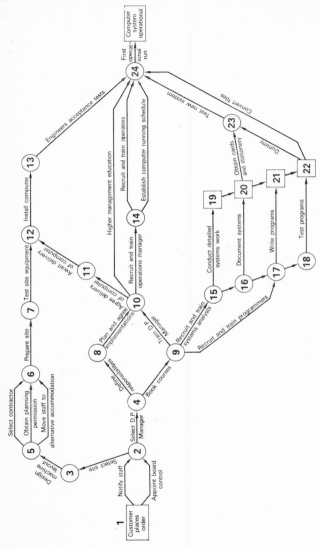

FIG. 13. A PERT network for installing a computer.

beginning or the end of an activity. In fact events are usually complex, representing the end of one or more activities and the beginning of one or more others. Events are particularly significant to management in that they represent the achievement of some objective.

Once the overall project has been broken down into a network of activities and events, values are given to each activity. Initially, an estimate of the duration of each activity is made. Once this has been done the estimated time of occurrence of each event can be calculated. This is done for each event by summing the times along the longest time path from the first event to the event in question. The longest time path from the first event to the last event is termed the critical path; the total of times along this path will be the time needed to complete the project. The probable time of occurrence of each event is also the time at which each activity may commence, bearing in mind the complex nature of events. If times along the longest time path from a given event to the last event are then added together, and the result subtracted from the expected completion date for the whole project, this will give the latest time at which an event may occur without extending the time needed to complete the whole project. If there is no difference between the probable time at which an event will occur and the latest time at which it may occur, then the event in question will be on the critical path. If these two times do not coincide, then the difference between them is said to be "slack" time for that event. It is possible to delay the event for the extent of the slack time without increasing the time taken to complete the project.

Associated with each activity will usually be a certain cost and an expenditure of resources of manpower and materials. When these requirements have been calculated, a detailed picture of the time and expense involved in the whole project is obtained. The network, in fact, can be considered as a model of the project, and as such manipulated to suit the particular objectives of management. There may be a deadline to meet which is exceeded by the estimated time needed to complete the project. If the project is the installation of a computer, this will mean that systems and programs may not be ready, and a large amount of capital in the form of a computer will be lying idle. In order to avoid this loss, the duration of certain activities on the critical path may be shortened by diverting resources to them, or resources may be increased. Since the critical activities have been isolated, management knows immediately to which activities attention should be given. Diverting resources from one activity to another may, however, cause other activities to become critical, and will in any case involve a recalculation of costs and the re-deployment of resources. In short, since activities are interrelated, adjustments to the values associated with any one of them may involve the recalculation of the whole network. Such a course is practical only with the aid of a computer. Given this aid, management may adjust the network until it suits specified objectives, whether these are concerned with time, cost, or the deployment of resources.

A complex project obviously stands a good chance of being successfully completed if it is thoroughly planned in this way. Such projects frequently take a long time to complete, however, and during this time the conditions under which the project was originally planned may change considerably. Shortages of manpower or materials may occur, or objectives in relation to time or cost may alter. There is therefore a need to control the progress of a complex project very closely, and the PERT network can be used to this end in the same way that it was used to plan the project. As each activity is completed, the actual amount of time, money, and resources used can be compared to the estimates, and totals accumulated. The detailed analysis of the effort expended on some activities may cause management to revise estimates for other activities. Moreover, this information can be summarized for all the completed activities, so that as each event is achieved management knows the total expenditure in time, money, and resources up to that time. With the aid of a computer, analyses of all the major factors affecting a project may be obtained in a matter of minutes. Such information may cause management to change its objectives from week to week; or if objectives are changed owing to external factors, management has up-to-the-minute information on the state of the project, and thus has the best chance of taking the most appropriate action. Indeed, various courses of action may be tried, and their effects simulated using the PERT network as a model, before any one course is selected to be put into practice. It can thus be seen that the PERT technique allows management a high degree of flexibility in planning and progressing any project.

CHAPTER 6

The Computer as a Decision Maker

MAKING decisions is one of the most important functions of a manager; the nature of decisions, and what making a decision involves, therefore bear some investigation. The decisions that a manager makes form part of a cyclical procedure which is illustrated in Fig.14. A manager makes a decision, taking into account the objectives that he is trying to achieve. As a result of his decision, some action is taken which affects the work that he controls; data indicating the effect of his decision is then collected and evaluated against the objectives that were to be achieved. Having assessed the effectiveness of his previous decision, the manager makes a new decision and the cycle is repeated.

By examining this cycle in more detail, the factors which have to be taken into account at each stage can be isolated, and the nature of a decision seen. The first consideration must be the objectives, since decisions are made in order to achieve something. Unless objectives are clearly defined, the manager can have little idea of what is required of him; objectives must therefore be specified in all relevant details. It is very uncommon in commercial situations for there to be one simple objective. A manager may be required to achieve a certain sales target, but there may be several constraints on how he is to do it. He will have to keep selling expenses within certain limits, and allocate sales effort taking into account not only the potential market but also distribution costs. He will also have to consider the penalties for not meeting the target, perhaps over-production and excessive inventory costs, or for exceeding the target, perhaps loss of goodwill through being unable to satisfy orders on time. Arising from this is the question of the degree of accuracy with which a target can be set. The target figure may be, for instance, 500 items, but the manager cannot be expected to meet this figure exactly; he needs to know the degree of variance from this figure, say a 5% variation, that is permissible before some form of penalty is incurred. Where several, often conflicting, objectives must be considered, the manager must know the relative importance of each objective. If possible, conflicting objectives should be given numeric values so that their relative importance is clearly defined, but this is frequently difficult to do in any meaningful way.

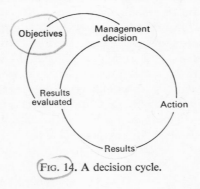

Fig. 14. A decision cycle.

Any decision presupposes two or more courses of action; if there is only one possible course of action then no decision has to be taken. A manager may worry about having to act in the only possible way, but it is pointless to waste time and effort in worrying about the inevitable. More frequently there will be a number of possible courses of action, and the manager will have another worry; whether he has considered them all. The difference between an adequate and a good manager can be that the former selects one of a number of standard courses of action while the latter is capable of innovation. The number of courses of action to be considered will often depend on the degree of detail with which each is defined, since any one course of action can usually be expanded into three or four by considering it in more detail. Thus, if possible courses of action are defined in great detail there is likely to be a large number from which to choose, making choice difficult: once a choice has been made, however, it should be relatively easy to implement since it is defined in detail. If, on the other hand, possible courses of action are not defined in detail, the opposite conditions will apply; there will be few possibilities, making choice easier, but the chosen course of action will be difficult to implement since it is not clearly defined.

Once the courses of action open to a manager have been established, he needs to have some criterion by which to judge their relative merits. Thus he needs to know the possible outcomes of any course of action, and the probability of any one of these outcomes occurring. Given this information, the manager can then choose the course of action which has the highest probability of producing the results that will enable him to achieve his objectives.

All these considerations should be taken into account in the making of a rational decision. When the decision has been implemented, and data on the effects of the chosen course of action becomes available, the manager examines the significant data in order to assess the effects of his decision. The information he obtains may cause him to modify his objectives, or they may be changed externally; they may, of course, remain the same, and if the manager's decision has proved fully effective, and circumstances have not changed, the manager may decide to take no further action for the moment. It must be appreciated, however, that even taking no action constitutes a decision, and can have just as important consequences as a more dramatic decision. Thus, whatever the manager does, the decision cycle is repeated.

Given the complex nature of decisions, how far is it possible to automate them, and, indeed, the whole decision cycle? Man has for many years used mechanized decision cycles, often termed servo-mechanisms. A simple example of a servo-mechanism is a thermostat. The objective of the decision cycle is defined by setting the regulator on, for instance, a heating system to a given temperature, say 60°F. The decision cycle shown previously can now be adapted as in Fig. 15 to show how the thermostat operates. The decision cycle for the thermostat follows exactly the same course as that of the management decision. The difference in the case of the thermostat is that the number of possible decisions is very small, the conditions requiring each decision clearly defined, and the infoimation as to which condition prevails exact and easy to obtain. This difference is fundamental, for upon it depends what can or cannot be automated. Analogue computers have for many years been used for process control; they react, in a similar way to

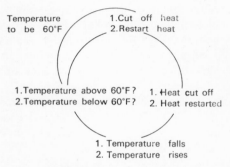

Temperature to be 60°F

1. Cut off heat
2. Restart heat

1. Temperature above 60°F?
2. Temperature below 60°F?

1. Heat cut off
2. Heat restarted

1. Temperature falls
2. Temperature rises

FIG. 15. Decision cycle in a thermostat.

the thermostat, to pressures, and temperatures arising in industrial processes, and cause valves to be opened or closed, or some other action to be taken to control the process in a predetermined manner. Although analogue computers are far more complex than thermostats, and can control very complicated processes, the basic conditions concerning the information to which they react are the same. The information concerns physical states that can be accurately and relatively easily measured.

Unfortunately, the manager in a commercial organization rarely receives such definite information. Just how definite the information he receives is will depend on, among other things, in which division of the company he works. Information about some commercial processes can be given in a quite definite form; little is known about other processes, so that the manager has less definite information on which to base his decisions. In neither case will information be as definite as in industrial process control, since it does not concern physical states. Nevertheless, in such commercial areas as production, finance, and accounting, much of the information is in a fairly definite form. The capacity of equipment in the production line is known, and the efficiency of production departments can be clearly seen; bottle-necks are equally apparent, and their causes not difficult to ascertain; and the volume of production is a set numeric quantity. Similarly, in finance and accounting, managers deal with figures that have a readily apparent meaning; there is no mystery about customers' balances, nor about why they show the figures that they do; neither is it difficult to establish whether a company is solvent or not. What all these divisions of a company have in common is that the human factor involved in their work is minimal. Marketing, on the other hand, involves selling to people, and customers are in no way as predictable or as easily quantifiable as production lines or accounts. It is because the human element in marketing is so strong that computers have until now been used less in this aspect of a company's work than in many others.

It is opportune at this point in the argument to reconsider the way in which digital computers operate. The digital computer manipulates values represented in the binary convention by a series of 0's and 1's. The computer makes decisions by being programmed to compare two values; any number of values may be compared by comparing successive pairs. A branch is made to a certain course of action according to whether one value is greater than, equal to, or less than the other. In the example given in Fig. 16 it is required to find the greatest of three unequal values A, B, and C; according to which value is greatest, a branch must then be made to D, E, or F respectively.

It follows from this that the various factors affecting any process which is to be controlled by a digital computer must be capable of being given a value. If the value of one factor in relation to other factors is not known, then the process cannot be programmed for control by a computer. Thus, processes which involve known values, such as production, finance, and accounting, can be placed under computer control relatively easily; where values are difficult to ascertain, considerable effort must be expended in order to discover them so that advantage can be taken of the computer's speed, accuracy, and "memory" capacity. In the past great credit has been attached to the qualities of experience and

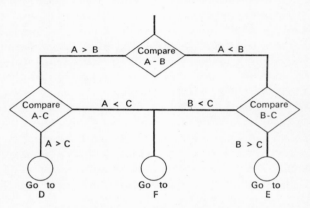

FIG. 16. A computer program decision structure.

intuition, and sometimes rightly so. Close examination of a manager's work, however, will reveal that very few of his decisions owe anything to intuition, or are in any way based on a mystical form of experience. Most of his decisions are based on knowledge of the job gained through practising it over a period of time, this being known as experience. Much of this knowledge will have been gained by rational deduction from observing the operation of the company; but since the process is rational, it can be stated in terms of "laws", and represented in mathematical terms. The fact that a manager has acquired certain knowledge through practical experience over a period of time does not mean that this is the only way of acquiring such knowledge. Indeed, it is a very in-efficient way of acquiring it; and even having acquired it, the manager may not make the best use of it. Managers, being human, are quite as capable of being irrational as rational; any number of circumstances could cause a manager who habitually acts rationally to make a completely irrational decision. Therefore, given that a process can be rationalized, and the factors affecting it quantified, it is better that it should be automated by programming it for computer control.

This provokes the question, What becomes of the manager's function of making decisions? The answer is in three parts. Firstly, there are some aspects of commercial situations in which intuition still has to be used, either because a particular aspect is irrational or because the logic by which it operates has not yet been discovered; the practical effect in either case is the same, the manager has to sort it out himself. Secondly, although some processes are known to be rational, no method has as yet been found of adequately quantifying the values affecting them. For instance, although certain advertising media are known to reach predominantly certain types of people, the number of the audience reached who will be appreciably influenced by any advertisement can be only approximately estimated. Thirdly, the number of possible reasons for a given situation occurring may be so large and so widely different that it is impractical or uneconomical to try to automate the reaction that should be made to the situation. This gives rise to an important concept in modern management, namely management by exception.

Suppose that the sales manager expects a certain salesman to attain a sales target of 500 items of a certain product. The computer record for that salesman will then contain the target figure of 500; since it is not possible to estimate targets exactly, and insignificant variations may occur, a general variation parameter of 5% may be included for all salesmen. Any variation within 5% of the target would be considered insignificant. Any variation of over 5%, however, requires action to be taken, although precisely what action will depend on the cause of the variation. There are many reasons why a salesman may fail significantly to reach his target, and a large proportion of these reasons may concern human problems. Whereas it is relatively easy to establish definite reasons why a production line has not met its expected target, it is much more difficult to establish why a salesman has failed to sell. In these circumstances it is more practical to have the computer merely bring the facts to the notice of the manager, and let him sort the problem out. A flowchart illustrating how this would be programmed on a computer is given in Fig. 17. It is worth noting

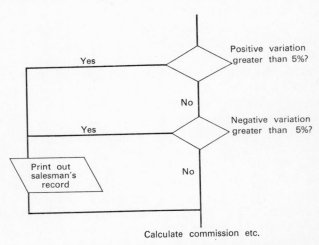

FIG. 17. Flowchart to print out exception conditions.

that some decisions are automated while others are not. The decision whether to print out the salesman's record, for instance, is included in the computer program; once the program has decided that the salesman's record should be printed out, however, it is left to the manager to decide what has caused the salesman to miss his target. It should be noted that the salesman's record will also be printed out if he exceeds his target by more than a given amount. A manager who is intent on gaining close control of his sales force will be just as interested in a positive variation as in a negative variation from expectations. If the manager can ascertain why the salesman exceeded his target, he may gain information that will enable him to increase sales generally. Thus management by exception involves inserting parameters in a program that will enable routine conditions, or insignificant variations from the norm, to be recognized and dealt with by the program. Significant variations, which can be dealt with more effectively by the manager, are printed out for his attention. Thus both the computer and the manager are allowed to do what each does most effectively.

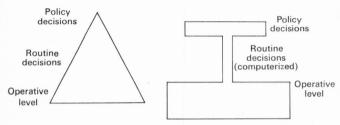

FIG. 18. Present and likely future hierarchical structure of companies.

The line between the decisions that are best automated and those best left to the manager is constantly changing, particularly in the work of the marketing manager. It was stated earlier that fewer decisions were automated in marketing than in other company divisions because of the difficulty of establishing definite information on market processes. Nevertheless, more and more research is being done into the processes by which markets operate, and as these processes become better understood so that the various factors affecting then can be isolated and quantified, so it will be increasingly possible to automate marketing decisions. Decisions which are now made by managers will become routine matters under computer control; only exceptional conditions will be brought to the manager's attention, and he will have more time to use his intuition and experience on the aspects of his work on which they are truly of value, aspects which are imperfectly understood and demand an acquired "sixth sense".

The impact of the computer as a decision maker will tend to change the traditional hierarchical structure of companies, as illustrated in Fig. 18. The pyramidical structure which prevails today will tend to change into a dumb-bell structure. Managers will be increasingly freed from routine work and will be able to concentrate on what are currently considered marginal aspects of their work. Management should thus become increasingly creative —an art as well as a science.

PART III

Use of the Computer in Marketing

CHAPTER 7

Inventory Control

THE basic questions associated with the control of an inventory are how much to order, and when? Assuming that demand and the time taken for an order of stock to be delivered are constant, the time to re-order will be at a point such that the order is delivered when existing stocks are exhausted. This is illustrated in Fig. 19.

In practice neither demand nor the time taken for an order of stock to be delivered will ever be absolutely constant. If both of these factors exceed expectation in one cycle, stocks will be exhausted before the replenishment order arrives, and customer service will suffer. If both factors are less than expected, considerable overstocking may result. The result of these variations is shown in Fig. 20. Since such variations will occur in practice, they must be considered, and this makes an inventory policy with a fixed re-order point undesirable. Revision of the re-order point involves a large amount of calculation, however, so that on normal manual systems such revisions cannot be very frequent. Given the use of a computer, however, frequent revisions of the re-order point involve only a minimum of effort. Thus re-order points can be calculated to take into account current trends in and estimates of demand.

Included in the re-order point will be a buffer level of stock. Buffer stock is held to allow for inaccuracies in estimates of demand, and its level will depend on the degree of accuracy with which demand can be forecast and the degree of service which is to be provided for customers. Evidently, a high level of buffer stock will ensure against stock-outs, and enable customers requirements always to be met from existing stocks. The cost of holding such a high level of stock is likely to be uneconomic, however, so that management will have to decide on a compromise that will enable the goodwill of customers to be kept while incurring the occasional stock-out. Once the level of buffer stock has been decided, it can be calculated automatically as a function of the variable re-order point.

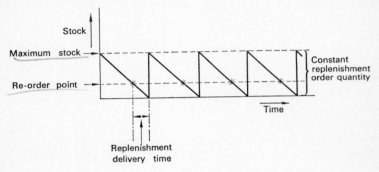

*Order placed here

Fig. 19. Stock picture of constant demand and replenishment time.

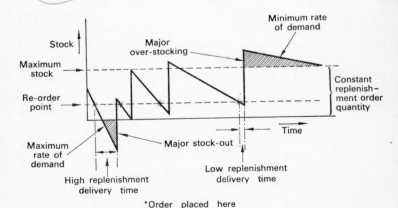

*Order placed here

Fig. 20. Variation of stock with variable demand and replenishment time.

Even with the re-order point established, it still remains to determine the level of stock which should be held. The level of stock to be held will define the quantity of stock to be re-ordered every time that the re-order point is reached, and the quantity ordered will in turn determine the frequency of re-ordering. The two conflicting factors to be optimized when deciding the re-order quantity are the cost of placing and receiving orders, which will rise in direct proportion to the frequency of orders, and the cost

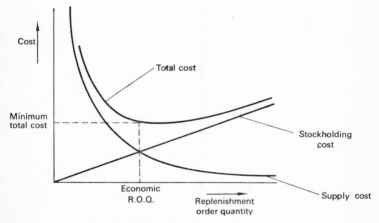

FIG. 21. Effect of order quantity on cost.

of holding large quantities of stock, which will necessarily result from infrequent orders. The relationship between these two conflicting costs is illustrated in Fig. 21; it can be seen that the sum of these two costs is lowest when the two costs are equal. The quantity of stock corresponding to this cost figure is thus the most economic re-order quantity.

An inventory control system embodying the principles outlined above involves a large amount of calculation and constant revision. As has already been indicated, the amount of calculation involved could not feasibly be carried out at frequent intervals by manual methods, so that any greater control gained through having detailed information would be lost because the time taken to obtain it would make it out of date. It would therefore be necessary to use a computer in order to extract the full benefit that can be derived from an adaptive inventory control system.

A typical inventory control computer system would include two principal parts; a series of analytical routines to establish from historical data the characteristics of stock items and to determine suitable control parameters, and a series of updating and forecasting routines to establish the current stock position, indicate which items needed replenishing, and forecast the future demand from current demand figures. The use of a computer would render most of these processes automatic; routine updating and adjustments would be done as a matter of course, and only exceptional conditions would be printed out for the attention of management.

In the first place management will have to make available appropriate historical and other data to be analysed. This data will include such information as the cost and sales price of items of stock, and the current amount of stock being held; in addition, historical data on the demand for items will have to be provided, and management will have to select the desired service level for the calculation of buffer stock, and an appropriate lead time for the replenishment of stock. The analytical routines might first establish the characteristics of items of stock so that management could decide which items were most suitable for inclusion in the inventory control computer system. It is probable that the requisite information will be difficult or impossible to obtain in the case of some items, while other items may not show a significant potential gain from close control, or may for other reasons be unsuitable for inclusion in the system. Subsequent analysis would establish such factors as seasonality and trend, and compute for each item or group of items a suitable demand forecasting frequency, prediction control parameter, and order quantity. When all the control parameters have been established, levels of buffer stock and total stock for each item can be calculated, and these figures totalled to give management an overall stock picture. Evidently, management could try the effects of various policies by

SYSTEM PERFORMANCE SUMMARY TABLE 1.			DATE 01/07/66			PAGE 8
SERVICE LEVEL GROUP		1	2	3	4	TOTAL
SERVICE LEVEL %		90.0	95.0	97.0	99.0	
NUMBER OF ITEMS IN GROUP		123.0	788.0	98.0	18.0	1027.0
SAFETY STOCK						
SAFETY STOCK AT COST	£	893.1	6967.2	685.5	139.1	8684.9
AVERAGE ANNUAL SALES AT COST	£	79188.3	653586.4	69527.2	15881.8	818183.7
SAFETY STOCK TURNOVER RATIO		88.7	93.8	101.4	114.2	94.2
TOTAL CURRENT STOCK HOLDING	£	3521.2	29388.0	2870.8	583.8	36363.8
AT MINIMUM STATISTICAL ORDERING INTERVAL						
TOTAL AVERAGE STOCK	£	1731.2	13413.0	1403.8	301.5	16849.5
TURNOVER RATIO		45.7	48.7	49.5	52.7	48.6
NUMBER OF ORDERS PER YEAR		5821.0	40001.0	4753.0	883.0	51458.0
AT PREFERRED ORDERING INTERVAL						
TOTAL AVERAGE STOCK	£	1931.2	15112.7	1576.3	301.5	18921.7
TURNOVER RATIO		41.0	43.2	44.1	52.7	43.2
NUMBER OF ORDERS PER YEAR		4691.0	31615.0	3853.0	883.0	41042.0
USING ECONOMIC REORDER QUANTITY FORMULA: BASED ON INVESTMENT RATE OF 20.0% & ORDERING COST OF £ .20						
TOTAL AVERAGE STOCK	£	2932.8	22715.8	2687.9	487.3	28823.8
TURNOVER RATIO		27.0	28.8	25.9	32.6	28.4
NUMBER OF ORDERS PER YEAR		2040.0	15749.0	2002.0	348.0	20139.0
SUM OF ROOT (YBAR X COST PRICE)		2884.6	22272.1	2831.8	492.5	28481.0

FIG. 22. Printout of summary of system performance analysis.

adjusting the control parameters before selecting the most suitable policy. The results of these analyses could be printed out in various ways, and one such printout is illustrated in Fig. 22. This printout gives an analysis of the expected performance of the current system selected against statistics derived by the analytical routines. If the performance was unsatisfactory, management could choose another system.

Once the original analyses have been performed, these routines are likely to be used again only if management wishes to review

ITEM NUMBER	ITEM DESCRIPTION	UNIT OF MEASURE	STOCK ON ORDER	STOCK ON HAND	REORDER POINT	REORDER QUANTITY	LEAD TIME	CYCLE IND.	SUPPLIER CODE	INC. MARK
A33	FLOUR SELF RAIS	BAGS	73	322	417	470	2	26	5A	1
C08	CHAPPIE LARGE	CASE	20	51	80	70	3	1	13C	1
D72	NESQUICK 8OZ	DOZ	31	258	300	328	2	52	10B	1
E13	KATTOMEAT	CASE	101	41	156	141	2	1	5C	1
E17	TIDYSAN 16 X 10	DOZ	122	81	208	224	3	1	3E	1
G22	TOP CAT HANDY	CASE	38	31	75	62	2	1	1F	1
J33	BONIOS SMALL	CASE	21	30	60	58	1	1	1C	1
K19	SHAPES	CASE	17	41	58	50	1	1	2C	1
L01	KATKINS	CASE	11	71	87	76	2	1	7F	1
M17	CAT FOOD PAWS	CASE	45	73	129	106	1	1	9F	1
.	.	.	.	.	.	.	.	.	.	.

REPLENISHMENT ORDER LIST   DATE 01/07/66   PAGE 1

Fig. 23. Printout of stock replenishment order list.

the performance of the system, or revise the system in some way, possibly by adding items to the inventory.

The remaining routines will concern updating and forecasting, and these will be run at suitable intervals decided by management. Thus far the objective has been to establish a viable control system by calculating suitable control parameters. This control system would then be merged with a stock master file; as transactions were processed against the stock master file, a comparison would be made between the updated stock figures and the re-order point for each item to ascertain whether replenishment of stock was necessary. If this were the case, an order for a suitable quantity of each item of stock, calculated according to the estimated demands for the coming period, and to any relevant control parameters, would be issued. Any stock deficiencies and other exceptional information would be printed out for management attention. A printout of a stock replenishment order list is shown in Fig. 23.

ITEM NUMBER	ITEM DESCRIPTION	STOCK ON HAND	STOCK ON ORDER	DEMAND LAST PERIOD	FORECAST LAST PERIOD	FORECAST INTERVAL
D52	INST. COFFEE	48	82	203	78	1
H17	CREAM STERIL	84	128	195	142	2
J32	SPECIAL MILK	21	93	151	88	1
J64	KENNOMEAT LARGE	17	221	201	105	1
M39	CHOC DROPS	87	96	273	152	1
O31	TOP CAT HANDY	111	106	197	138	1
P72	LASSIE LARGE	38	51	84	39	1
.	.	.	.	.	.	.

REPORTED ITEMS LIST   DATE 01/07/66   PAGE 1

Fig. 24. Printout of a reported items list.

The forecasting routines would be used to bring forecasts of demand up to date. A new predicted demand for the next period would be computed taking into account the demand over the previous period, the error between that demand and the fore-casted demand, and any seasonality factor that might be present. At the same time a new re-order point and quantity would be calculated for each item. Items for which the estimated demand during the previous period was significantly different from the actual demand would be printed out as exceptional conditions for the attention of management. A printout of a reported item list is shown in Fig. 24.

An inventory control computer system such as the one that has been described will fit unobtrusively into the general framework of a company's system. The largest part of the effort involved is in initially establishing the control system; once this has been done, the control routines can be run at the same time as the normal stock updating routines, and control of the overall stock position will be taken care of with only exceptional conditions being brought to the attention of management. Management can then investigate these conditions and take appropriate action, adjusting the control system if this is necessary. An adaptive inventory control system will thus relieve management of a good deal of routine work, and require only occasional attention, leaving management to concentrate on the currently important aspects of the inventory.

CHAPTER 8

Sales Accounting

UNDER this general heading of sales accounting a typical computer system for invoicing, sales ledger, and sales analysis will be described. Since the information required for all three processes is similar, one comprehensive system would normally be designed to include procedures for all the processes. Invoicing and sales ledger produce no information that is important to management; the processes have to be carried out, however, and advantages can be gained from having them computerized. Sales analysis, on the other hand, provides essential management information, particularly in markets where competition is fierce, and close control of the marketing effort consequently vital. Detailed analyses of sales figures should indicate to management trends in the market as regards customers, areas, and types of product, and should also provide information to help in the control of salesmen.

If the inventory of a company is controlled by means of a computer system, incoming orders will usually be processed against the stock master file first of all in order to update the inventory. Supposing that this is the case, extra items of information needed for invoices will be copied from the stock master file so that the orders will be expanded before being written to magnetic tape, or any other medium, during the inventory updating run. Information that might be needed from the master stock file for invoicing includes the price of the product, and any restrictions on the quantities that may be ordered; for instance, only dozens. When the original orders have been expanded in this way and written to tape, they will be sorted by the computer to customer account number sequence ready for invoicing.

The magnetic tape containing the customer account file will then be loaded on to a tape deck, and processed against the expanded orders in order to make available the information necessary for the invoices to be printed out. The customer accounts file will contain all relevant particulars of the customer, including the category in which he is classed, and discounts or special terms to which he is entitled. This information will be used in the calculation of debits to his account on the invoice. Details of incoming cash transactions may have been included on the original orders

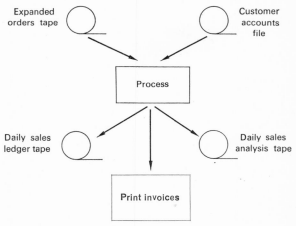

FIG. 25. Invoicing run.

tape; if not, they can be added in a separate computer run before the sales ledger master tape is updated. In Fig. 25, it is assumed that cash transactions are already on the orders tape. Three lots of output will be produced from the invoicing run; the invoices will be printed, and this data in addition to the cash transactions will be copied to the daily sales ledger tape; details of sales will be copied to another tape for sales analysis purposes. If the inventory of outgoing products is run on a first-in-first-out (FIFO) basis, a control feature can be included on invoicing. To ensure that the FIFO system is adhered to, a sequence number can be printed against products on the invoice, having been copied previously from the stock master file. This will prevent warehousemen from working an unofficial LIFO system, with the consequent risk of stock deterioration. Data on the daily sales analysis tape will include the type of customer, the salesman's number, and the sales area, as well as the number and type of product ordered.

When the invoicing run has been completed, the sales ledger run can be set up by loading the sales ledger master file. The master file holds details of all invoices sent out during the month and,

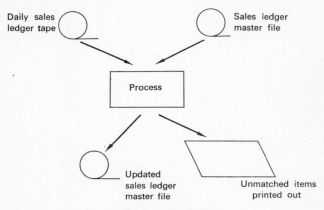

Daily sales ledger tape

Sales ledger master file

Process

Updated sales ledger master file

Unmatched items printed out

FIG. 26. Daily sales ledger run.

additionally, details of items outstanding from earlier periods. The purpose of the daily sales ledger run (Fig. 26) is to copy the day's invoices to the sales ledger master file and to delete transactions on the master file that are accounted for by the day's cash transactions. It frequently happens that payments and debited items cannot be matched, in which case the relevant details will be printed out by the computer so that appropriate action can be taken. These transactions can be included in a following day's run when they have been properly matched. At the end of each period the sales ledger master file will be processed against the customer accounts file in order to produce periodical statements, notices of payments overdue, and any other such documentation that may be required. Transactions which have been settled will be written to a tape to be used for audit purposes, and the sales ledger master file will be left with only incompleted transactions to be carried forward to the next period.

The sales analysis tape produced on the invoicing run is built up day by day until the end of the period. The data on this tape can then be sorted by the computer to a variety of sequences and

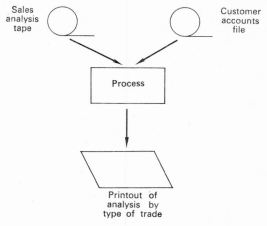

Fig. 27. Daily sales analysis run.

used in conjunction with other tapes to produce the desired analyses. For instance, the sales analysis tape (Fig. 27) could first be sorted to type of product within salesman number within sales area sequence. The tape could then be processed against a sales master file holding historical sales data to produce various printouts. One printout might show a comparison between the current period's sales figures, and the corresponding figures for the previous period and the same period of the previous year. A comparison with the expected demand for the period could also be made, and both sets of data could then be used in the sales forecasting procedures required for the adaptive inventory control. At the same time, the commission due to salesmen could be calculated, and the figures produced used as a measure for controlling the sales force. By sorting the sales analysis tape to customer number sequence and processing it against the customer accounts file, further useful analyses could be produced. Analyses by customer and type of trade compared with similar historical data might indicate trends in specific areas of the market, and suggest adjustments to the apportionment and distribution of the sales effort. Any number of analyses may be made, during which the sales master file will be updated and the daily sales tape cleared for use in accumulating the following period's sales figures.

The reader should now have a clear idea of the way in which data which has relevance to a number of aspects of a company's work can be used to provide accurate and detailed information rapidly with the aid of a computer. The above description shows how the various processes of invoicing, sales ledger and analysis, and inventory control are to some extent dependent for their control on the same data. The greater the degree in which the systems by which a company carries out its work are integrated, the more use a computer can be. Since, in a computer system, large volumes of information can be rapidly edited and sorted to any desired form, it is possible to think in terms of one single store of data from which any information required for any of the company's functions can be drawn and used with the minimum of duplication and the maximum flexibility.

CHAPTER 9

Credit Control

THE major problem associated with credit control is to interpret a credit policy in terms of concrete figures. To say that a customer is a good credit risk or a bad credit risk is meaningless unless the standards on which such a judgement is based are known. Similarly, if a manager is told to tighten or loosen credit, how is he to interpret this policy in terms of individual customers? In practice the decision whether or not to allow credit, or how much to allow, is most frequently based to a considerable extent on the intuition of the person making the decision.

Some customers, or potential customers, will show clear signs of being either good or bad credit risks; the large majority, however, will require a certain amount of assessment. In these cases, a credit policy is likely to be applied with too much rather than too little caution. If a customer accumulates debts which have to be written off, the mistake is obvious to all concerned and the blame will be attributed to the manager responsible for allowing the credit in the first place. If, on the other hand, a customer who may be considered a definite risk is allowed credit and meets his commitments in full and on time, perhaps nobody other than the credit manager, who can then breathe more freely, will ever notice. In these circumstances the credit manager may have more to gain by being over-cautious than he has by trying to extend his credit trade.

Nevertheless, each potential customer turned down as a bad credit risk is trade lost. A company offering credit therefore has to set the larger volume of trade associated with a "loose" credit policy against the greater number of debts which will probably have to be written off. The problem facing management is to optimize this situation, and in order to do this detailed and exact information on what constitutes a good or bad credit risk is necessary.

This much has been realized for some time; the problem has been how to obtain such information without excessive cost and effort. A frequently used technique involves the formulation of a questionnaire, the answers to each question being given a weight designed to produce a score which will indicate the suitability of the applicant to be allowed credit. The difficulty has been to find the right questions to ask and the correct weight for each answer, since these factors often change considerably with time and from area to area. Another difficulty lies in the selection of a passing score, since this should presuppose a knowledge of the probable effects, in terms of profit and loss, of any passing score chosen. The effort involved in obtaining enough information to evolve and maintain a rational credit policy has generally been considered impractical, with the result that most credit policies have been based largely on intuition.

With the advent of computers and special purpose programs supplied by the machine manufacturer, particularly facilities for statistical analysis, information retrieval, and simulation, the amount of effort required for a rational credit policy has been considerably reduced. Historical data concerning personal details of customers who have been allowed credit, together with details of their accounts, can be collected and analysed to establish the characteristics which have had a critical bearing on their credit performance. Much of the required data may already be available in sales accounting files. Where questionnaires have been formulated intuitively there is a frequent tendency to ask too many questions, some of which are irrelevant. A statistical analysis should help establish the factors that are directly relevant to the credit worthiness of customers, and thus will in many cases eliminate superfluous work by reducing the size of the questionnaire. At the same time the relative importance of each chacteristic can be estimated and given an appropriate weight. In this way a scoring scale can be established and applied to a representative selection of customers who have in the past proved good credit risks, and also to a similar selection who have proved bad credit risks. The scores obtained by good and bad risks can be illustrated as in Fig. 28.

It can be seen that the passing score that will optimize credit trade must lie somewhere along the bottom line in the shaded area. To the left of the shaded area lie scores obtained by what have proved only bad risks; to the right of the shaded area lie scores

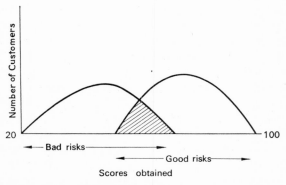

FIG. 28. Scores obtained by good and bad credit risks.

obtained only by good risks. The passing score selected will depend on the objectives of the credit policy, so that in order to decide on any given score management must know what the results of choosing such a score will be. A model of the credit situation can be constructed using current information on the income from credit, and the expenses in debts which have to be written off. The results of different credit policies can then be simulated. Moreover, any given policy, whether to maximize profit or to keep the total amount of credit allowed below a certain limit, will correspond to a certain passing score.

Therefore, instead of a vague directive to tighten or loosen credit policy to an intuitive degree, a change in policy can be stated as a directive to higher or lower the passing score by a definite number of points. In this way changes in credit policy can be more subtle, and will not be open to misinterpretation. If necessary, different policies can be established for different areas, and all policies can be revised at appropriate intervals with comparatively little extra effort. None of this would be feasible without the aid of a computer and the special purpose software obtained with it.

A rational credit policy can also be of great benefit in a large retail outlet, such as a big departmental store, where computer facilities are available. Apart from the general credit problem described earlier, there are special problems associated with the granting of credit facilities in a big store. If the credit policy is intuitive, a large number of customers may have to be interviewed before credit can be allowed. This involves keeping somebody at managerial level permanently available to give interviews, and means that potential customers can be subjected to an embarrassingly long wait.

However, if there is a clearly defined credit policy, and either a computer within the store or a line connected to a computer owned by the company, then several advantages can be obtained. In the first place, as stated earlier, a short questionnaire may suffice to obtain the required information from the potential customer. This information can then be transmitted by internal telephone from any department within the store to where the computer facilities are available; the computer can be interrogated and a score for the customer obtained in a matter of seconds. The whole operation should not take more than a few minutes. Thus customers need not be subjected to long waits, sales staff can concentrate on their job of selling rather than making initial appraisal of customers and deciding whether to refer them to the manager and the manager will have to conduct relatively few interviews and so can concentrate on the business of management.

CHAPTER 10

Market Research

MARKET research has for a long time been associated with the use of computers. Organizations such as the A. C. Neilsen company handle extremely large volumes of data which have to be analysed in a very short time if the information obtained is to be of practical use. In a given survey cycle over a million cards have to be punched and thousands of tables and hundreds of reports produced. This is possible only with the aid of electronic equipment. The need for a computer in such circumstances requires no further explanation; the following discussion will therefore concern itself with the establishment of a market file by companies for which market research is only a part of their sales effort.

The object of a market file built up and maintained by individual companies is to have to hand information on the market or markets in which they are interested, and to be able to assess their own performance and decide in which areas of the market sales effort can most profitably be concentrated. A starting point for establishing a marketing file would be to obtain from current sales data an analysis by trade and type of customer of the outlets for a particular product. This information will generally be of practical value only if the possible outlets for a product are restricted to some extent; if a product has too general a use the number and type of outlets will provide little useful information, and will involve the processing of very large volumes of data.

Information from sales data will reveal only the existing market in which the company has been successful. If data on past customers is available, this too could be analysed and added to the data on current customers. However, if the market file being established is to prove of long-term value in providing marketing information, data on potential customers must be included as well. Certain inferences can usually be drawn from the analyses of existing customers. For instance, if the product being marketed is used in large scale financial procedures, one would expect to find large groups of current customers in banking and insurance. A reference to commercial or other directories will then reveal lists of companies in the same field of business as current customers, and which can reasonably be considered as potential customers. In this way a list of outlets in both the existing and potential market can be built up, punched into cards, and written to magnetic tape. The computer will be of no help in searching through directories to find the potential market unless the directories are obtainable in some machine sensible form. It can be used for the analysis of existing customers, however, and will prove of further use later.

Having established the market, an attempt must be made to assess the usage of the product in question. The sort of information that is required is the number and type of the product being used, and from where supplies were obtained. These details will be known for existing customers, and if this sample was a sufficiently large and representative proportion of the whole market, the data could be expanded statistically to infer the probable usage among potential customers. It is likely, however, that the sample of existing customers will not be such as to allow accurate inferences to be drawn. It will therefore be necessary to find some means of obtaining the required information.

The means chosen will depend largely on the product in question, since this will determine the availability of the information. Trade journals and organizations may provide some of the information. Questionnaires can be drawn up and sent to potential customers, although this method is subject to some limitations. Questionnaires are most practical where it is required to obtain a small amount of information from a large number of people, since if little effort is required, more people are likely to return the questionnaires. Even so, after repeated postings, the number of replies received may not exceed 50 %. If this coverage is sufficient, then questionnaires provide a cheap means of obtaining information. Another possibility is to simply phone potential customers, although this would be practical only if the number of potential customers were not too large. Either of the last two means described may encounter some resistance if the potential customers think they are being involved in some selling line. To avoid this, an agency could be hired to obtain the desired information. Finally, salesmen can themselves note the usage of the product when going on their usual rounds.

When sufficient information has been obtained, it can be punched into cards and transferred on to magnetic tape. It is at this point that a computer becomes extremely useful. The two tapes, one holding details of each customer or potential customer, and the other holding details of usage of the product and from whom it was obtained, can now be sorted and merged to form the market file. Merging the data would involve a great deal of time and effort if done manually, but is a simple and rapid operation if a computer is used. The value of the market file will naturally depend on the degree to which the information in it is accurate and complete. Once the initial information has been obtained it should be possible to update the file by means of statistical probability, and here again the aid of a computer will save time and cost.

With the market file established, a number of analyses may be made, as with sales data for sales statistics. Analyses by area and type of customer will reveal the sections of the market in which the company is strongest and weakest. Sections of the market where usage of the product has not been fully exploited should also be revealed. Thus management can obtain information on how best to distribute the sales effort according to the type of customer and geographical location. The market file should, moreover, provide a guide to the company's performance in relation to other companies competing in the same market. Information retrieval software may also be used in conjunction with the market file to provide mailing lists of customers of a certain type or in a certain area. As with the sales analysis file, given the aid of computer hardware and software, the market file can be used to provide essential information rapidly and relatively cheaply, and thus facilitate more effective deployment of marketing resources.

CHAPTER 11

Delivery

A PROBLEM facing every sales manager is that of distribution. Given a number of supply points, which may be factories, for instance, and a number of demand points, which may be wholesale stores, the sales manager needs to know how goods can be transported from the supply to the demand points at the minimum cost. The problem may be complicated by the presence of intermediate points, such as warehouses, at which goods are received from factories before being further distributed.

This sort of problem is often tackled by clerks, who choose the cheapest distribution routes first of all, and then successively more expensive routes until all the demand has been satisfied. While this approach appears logical, it very often fails to provide the minimum cost solution; if there are more than a few supply and demand points, and if demand at one point is met in varying degrees from a number of supply points, the desired solution can be very difficult to find. Moreover, if demand varies to any great extent, the distribution network may need to be recalculated at frequent intervals, a task that can involve a considerable amount of effort if attempted by manual methods. Operational research specialists have therefore devised methods of solving this type of problem using an adaptation of the linear programming technique. The problem in its simplest form, without intermediate points, is known as the transportation problem; if intermediate points are present, it is known as the transhipment problem. Transhipment programs are supplied by computer manufacturers as part of the standard software. A transhipment program can be used for solving both transportation and transhipment problems; a simple example of the use of such a program is given below.

Suppose that supply points are located at Dover and Deal, intermediate points at London and Slough, and demand points at Leeds and York. In practice, many more points would probably have to be considered, but the approach to the problem would be essentially the same. The following information must be made available for input to the computer; the total supply at each of the supply points, the total requirements at each of the demand points, the maximum amount that can be carried along each route between any two points, and the cost of carriage on each route. The points, routes, and necessary input data are illustrated in Fig. 29. The numbers at Deal and Dover are the total supply and those

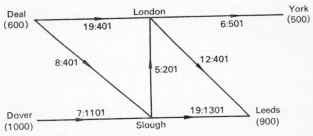

FIG. 29. A specimen transhipment network.

at York and Leeds the total demand. The numbers along each route are the unit cost of transportation along that route, followed by the transportation capacity in units.

Given this data, the program will calculate how the demand can be met, within the constraints of supply and transportation capacity, at a minimum cost. If there is no feasible solution, as would be the case if, for instance, demand were greater than supply, the program will print out the optimum solution within the limits of feasibility. The problem above, however, has a feasible solution, which is shown as it would be printed out by the computer in Fig. 30.

Only the routes selected in the solution are shown on the printout. The information given under the various headings is as follows. Under ROWNAM are listed the successive points from which goods are to be sent, under COLNAM the successive points at which goods are received. Thus goods must flow from Slough and Deal to London, from Dover and Deal to Slough, and so on. Under BOUND are listed the route capacity constraints, and under COST the unit cost associated with each route. The column FLOW gives the recommended quantities that should be transported along each route in order to provide the minimum cost solution. The figures in column COST FLOW are the products of COST and FLOW,

PRIMAL	SOLUTION							
ROWNAM	COLNAM	BOUND	COST	FLOW	COSTFLOW	RCOST	ALPHA	BETA
SLOUGH	LONDON	201	5	201	1005	−6	8	19
DEAL	LONDON	401	19	299	5681	0	0	19
SUM	LONDON				6686			
DOVER	SLOUGH	1101	7	1000	7000	0	1	8
DEAL	SLOUGH	401	8	101	808	0	0	8
SUM	SLOUGH				7808			
LONDON	YORK	501	6	500	3000	0	19	25
SUM	YORK				3000			
SLOUGH	LEEDS	1301	19	900	17100	0	8	27
SUM	LEEDS				17100			

FIG. 30. Computer printout of solution.

giving the cost associated with the flow of goods along each route included in the solution. These costs are summed for each of the intermediate and demand points. The sales manager is thus provided with the information that he needs; moreover, whenever any of the variables or constraints have their values changed, the program can be re-run and a new minimum cost solution obtained in a matter of seconds.

Certain extra information is provided on the printout, some of which may prove of interest to the sales manager; in particular column BETA, which shows marginal costs, may be noted. The figures in this column show the cost of transporting one extra unit of goods to each of the towns listed under COLNAM. Several points of interest emerge. The figure given for transporting one extra unit from Slough to London is 19, whereas on the original network the unit cost figure was 5. The reason for this change in cost is that the transportation capacity between Slough and London is already being fully used, so that any extra unit must be transported direct from Deal to London with the associated unit cost of 19. Similarly, the marginal cost given for the Dover to Slough route is 8, because the quantity available at Dover (1000) has been fully taken up, even though the route capacity (1101) is not fully utilized, so that the extra unit must come from Deal. This is why the marginal cost at Leeds is 27 and not 26. By studying the marginal costs, the sales manager can see where capacity is insufficient; in the problem illustrated, it is clear that considerable savings could be made if the supply capacity at Dover and the transportation capacity along the Slough to London route could be extended. By providing different supply and transportation constraints as input to the program, it would be possible to estimate the savings that could be made if capacity could be increased. Given the cost of increasing capacity, the sales manager could then decide whether this was a worth-while proposition. Alternatively, the sales manager could take some action to encourage increased sales at points where the marginal costs of supply were lowest. In any case, it can be seen that information on marginal costs can be of considerable use in planning the distribution of goods.

A transhipment program can also be used inversely to plot suitable locations for supply points, such as warehouses. In this case it is unlikely that the demand at individual towns would be considered, since finding or building warehouses is a long-term investment, and demand might change considerably. Demand would therefore be considered by area. This information, together with data on costs and capacity constraints, would enable the program to be used to select the approximate sites in which warehouses should be located in order to minimize distribution costs.

CHAPTER 12

Investment Appraisal

AN AREA in which frequent and sometimes costly errors are made is evaluation of investment opportunities. With rising competition and pressure on profit margins, companies are becoming less able to afford such errors. Nevertheless, investment decisions have constantly to be made if profits are to be maintained. In these circumstances management needs some more scientific method than following intuition in order to choose the projects in which a company should invest. Various methods of appraising the probable profitability of projects have been known for some time, but the amount of calculation involved has hindered their wide acceptance. However, computer software packages are available which enable a company to employ a number of techniques to assess the profitability of projects scientifically, while the computer copes rapidly with the repetitious and laborious calculations involved.

The investment problem can be broken down into a number of component parts. The changes in the cash flows which would result from implementing a given project must be calculated. This involves consideration of changes in working capital, tax grants, manufacturing and inventory costs, revenue from sales, and so on. The result of the sum of costs and revenue will give the net cash flow, which must be adapted in some way so that the profitability of one project can be compared to that of others. Evaluation of the profitability of a project must take into account the degree of certainty associated with any given profit figure. Other factors, such as welfare or prestige, may also have to be taken into account before projects can finally be compared in the light of company objectives, and a decision made as to which project or projects are to be implemented.

An investment appraisal software package might be used as follows. A company has devised a number of projects, including possibly new products to be launched, and wishes to know the relative profitability of each project in order to decide which of the projects should be implemented. Estimates of cash flows such as capital costs, manufacturing and inventory costs, and sales revenue have to be provided by management, as also do details of the investment and tax allowances and tax costs to be applied to each project. This data is punched into cards and input to the computer. The software package is then used to calculate the yearly or periodical state of each cash flow, and the profit from a given project at a given time. Evaluation of different projects may be on the basis of payback period, average annual rate of return, or a discounted cash flow (DCF) technique.

The problem of comparing the value of different projects can be stated briefly as the difficulty in comparing a project that will produce £A profit over B years and a project that will produce £X profit over Y years. In other words, how to relate the value of income to the time at which it is obtained. Clearly £10,000 profit in one year has not the same value as £10,000 5 years later. This difficulty is not always faced in estimates of the value of projects, possibly because of the amount of calculation involved, which could require significant effort if only manual methods of processing data were available. The payback period method of evaluating projects has the virtue of simplicity, but ignores the above problem.

The payback period is the number of years required to recover the capital invested in a project. The calculations involved are simple, but no account is taken of the amount of profit to be obtained after the payback period, nor is allowance made for the greater value of money in the early years of the payback period. The projects considered preferable are those that have the shortest payback period, but two projects with the same payback period may be given an equal status, which could be very misleading.

One project may, for instance, recover most of its capital in the early years of the payback period, while the other recovers most of its capital in the later years. This situation is illustrated in Fig. 31 and should give project A a higher status than project B. The average annual rate of return method of evaluating projects takes into account profit made after the payback period, but shares the drawback of not allowing for the greater value of money in the earlier years of the project's life.

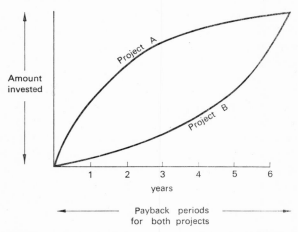

FIG. 31. Comparison of two projects with the same payback period.

DCF techniques have been evolved to cope with the problem of the value of money in relation to the time at which it is obtained. The basis of these techniques is the calculation of compound interest in reverse. The net present value DCF technique requires the selection of a discount rate, which may be the cost of capital or the amount which this capital is expected to earn. If the selected discount rate were 10%, it would be assumed that £100 capital at the current time would be worth £110 one year later, and £121 2 years later. On this assumption it can be stated that £121 obtained in 2 years' time has an equivalent value to £100 obtained now. In this way, money obtained over a period of time can be reduced to an equivalent current value, or net present value. Thus, taking the originally stated problem of comparing a project which makes £A profit in B years and a project which makes £X profit in Y years, these projects can be reduced to a common basis of having a net present value of £$A \div (10\%)^B$ and £$X \div (10\%)^Y$ respectively. Other DCF techniques involve refinements of this basic principle. The yield DCF technique, for instance, involves repeating the above calculations with different discount rates until a rate is found which causes positive and negative cash flows to be equal. This rate will be the rate of return on capital, which may be more meaningful to management than a net present value for a project. Other refinements are more complex, and need not be considered here.

If it is desired to include consideration of the accuracy of management's cash flow estimates, various estimates may be given for each type of cash flow associated with each project, and a probability factor assigned to each estimate. Estimates of the manufacturing costs of a project may vary, for instance, between £500,000 and £700,000. In this case, management would be required to assess the probability of each of the included estimates occurring, so that the total probability of all estimates was 1, or 100%. A probability factor must be supplied with each of the cash-flow estimates provided by management as input to the computer. The computer then calculates, in a number of runs, cash flows and other information such as the DCF field rate, selecting one of the estimates for each type of cash flow at a time so that number of times each estimate is selected corresponds to the probability of that estimate occurring. When the number of runs have been completed, a frequency distribution of the profit to be expected is printed out.

Using such a software package, management can have as simple or as sophisticated a system of assessing the value of investments as is required. A short computer run would provide management with information on the payback period of projects. Longer runs would provide a detailed evaluation of projects using DCF

PLANT EXPANSION – BRAND X.   ASSUMPTIONS – NO IN/DEFLATION OF COSTS/PRICES
GRANT 20%, ANNUAL ALL. 20%. REDUCING BALANCE FOR 5 YEARS. CORPORATION TAX 40%

YEAR	PERIOD	CAPITAL INVESTMENT	OTHER CAPITAL	INVESTMENT GRANT	INITIAL ALLOWANCE	ANNUAL ALLOWANCE	REVENUE INCOME	REVENUE COSTS	REVENUE PROFIT	TAX ON PROFIT	NET CASH FLOW
1966	3	=10000.0	0.0	0.0	0.0	0.0	0.0	-500.0	-500.0	0.0	-10500.0
	4	=2000.0	0.0	0.0	0.0	0.0	3000.0	-1000.0	2000.0	0.0	0.0
1967	1	0.0	0.0	0.0	0.0	0.0	2500.0	-1000.0	1500.0	0.0	1500.0
	2	0.0	0.0	0.0	0.0	0.0	2000.0	-1000.0	1000.0	0.0	1000.0
	3	0.0	0.0	0.0	0.0	640.0	3000.0	-1000.0	2000.0	-600.0	2040.0
	4	0.0	0.0	0.0	0.0	0.0	2500.0	-1000.0	1500.0	0.0	1500.0
1968	1	0.0	0.0	2000.0	0.0	0.0	2500.0	-1000.0	1500.0	0.0	3500.0
	2	0.0	0.0	0.0	0.0	0.0	2000.0	-1000.0	1000.0	0.0	1000.0
	3	0.0	0.0	0.0	0.0	512.0	3000.0	-1000.0	2000.0	-2400.0	112.0
	4	0.0	0.0	0.0	0.0	0.0	2500.0	-1500.0	1000.0	0.0	1000.0
1969	1	0.0	0.0	0.0	0.0	0.0	2000.0	-1500.0	500.0	0.0	1000.0
	2	0.0	0.0	0.0	0.0	0.0	2500.0	-1500.0	1000.0	0.0	500.0
	3	0.0	0.0	0.0	0.0	409.6	2500.0	-2000.0	500.0	-2200.0	-790.0
	4	0.0	0.0	0.0	0.0	0.0	0.0	0.0	0.0	0.0	500.0
1970	1	0.0	0.0	0.0	0.0	0.0	0.0	0.0	0.0	0.0	0.0
	2	0.0	0.0	0.0	0.0	0.0	0.0	0.0	0.0	0.0	0.0
	3	0.0	0.0	0.0	0.0	327.7	0.0	0.0	0.0	-1000.0	-672.3
	4	0.0	0.0	0.0	0.0	0.0	0.0	0.0	0.0	0.0	0.0
1971	1	0.0	800.0	0.0	0.0	0.0	0.0	0.0	0.0	0.0	800.0
	2	0.0	0.0	0.0	0.0	0.0	0.0	0.0	0.0	0.0	0.0
	3	0.0	0.0	0.0	0.0	1310.7	0.0	0.0	0.0	0.0	1310.7
	4	0.0	0.0	0.0	0.0	0.0	0.0	0.0	0.0	0.0	0.0
1972	1	0.0	0.0	0.0	0.0	0.0	0.0	0.0	0.0	0.0	0.0
	2	0.0	0.0	0.0	0.0	0.0	0.0	0.0	0.0	0.0	0.0
	3	0.0	0.0	0.0	0.0	-320.0	0.0	0.0	0.0	0.0	-320.0

FIG. 32. Printout showing net cash flow.

techniques and giving the probability of different levels of profit being obtained. Even in the more sophisticated uses of such a software package, all that is required of management is estimates of original cash flows and an assessment of the probability of each estimate occurring. From this basic data, the computer calculates the state of cash flows at each stage of the project's life, and provides management with the information required in the form of printouts. An example of a printout showing the net cash flow is given in Fig. 32. Relieved of tedious and sometimes complex calculations, management can concentrate on ensuring that its estimates are achieved and that the expected sales revenue is attained or exceeded.

CHAPTER 13

PERT Applied to Launching a New Product

A COMMON application of PERT which is of significance in the marketing field is to the launching of a new product. Once the product to be launched has been chosen, management is faced with a number of problems to resolve. A major factor in the profitability of the product will be the cost of producing it, so that close control of costs is essential; such control is not easy to achieve if the production processes are complex, and unforeseen difficulties can often seriously reduce the expected profit margin if the project is not properly planned. Another factor, perhaps even more important, is the time at which the product is launched; clearly, it is possible to guarantee a launching date only if the time needed for production can be accurately estimated, and tightly controlled to ensure that deadlines are met. If sales of the product are going to be subject to seasonality, even a week's delay could have a disastrous effect on profits. Moreover, if the selling campaign involves a gradual escalation of publicity over a long period of time prior to the product's being launched, failure to meet the production deadline can ruin a carefully planned publicity campaign costing perhaps hundreds of thousands of pounds. For these and other reasons, the close control afforded by the PERT technique can be of invaluable aid to management.

The first task facing management is to break down the overall project into activities over which it is desired to exercise control. In this way a network of related activities is constructed, as described in the earlier general account of the PERT technique.

The time and resources needed for each activity are then calculated. If activities are unfamiliar to the company it may not be possible to give time estimates with any degree of certainty. In this case, three time estimates can be made, and a suitably weighted average estimate taken. The average is commonly calculated according to the equation given below.

$$\text{Expected time} = \frac{\text{Optimistic estimate} + (4 \times \text{likely estimate}) + \text{pessimistic estimate}}{6}$$

Resources can be subject to a number of different specifications. The general categories in which resources are grouped are manpower, materials, and finance, although each of these can be specified in more detail. Constraints can be placed on the availability of resources, and the time at which given resources are required within the total time needed to complete an activity can also be specified. The availability of resources is elastic in that manpower, for instance, can be increased by allowing for shift work or overtime. The extra resources available in this way are known as threshold resources. Some resources, known as pool resources, can be transferred from one activity to a subsequent one if the amount allocated to the earlier activity is not fully utilized. An obvious example of a pool resource is money; specialized equipment, on the other hand, may only be utilizable for one given activity, and if the equipment is not used to the full, the excess capacity is simply wasted. The ability to define resources in detail allows management great flexibility when establishing possible schedules.

It is in the computation of schedules that the advantages of, and most frequently the necessity for, the aid of a computer are first seen. A network of about a hundred activities could be processed manually, although the computation of all feasible schedules would involve a large amount of repetitive, tedious, and hence error prone work. A network of a thousand activities, on the other hand, would be too large for manual processing to be a practical consideration; yet the same network could be input to a computer, checked, sorted, and analysed to produce a time schedule in a matter of minutes.

A typical method of computing schedules is to process the network first to establish the critical path and the amount of float time associated with each activity; resources are not considered. Schedules can then be computed assuming activities to start at their earliest possible starting date, and then at their latest possible starting date without extending the time needed to complete the overall project. If printouts were made of the allocation of resources necessary to achieve these schedules, it would be found in the former case that the distribution of the work load throughout the project was uneven, the demand on resources sometimes being very high, and the associated costs would be inflationary. There would be very little risk, however, of the project failing to meet its completion deadline. In the latter case the distribution of the work load would also be uneven, but the cost of the project may be reduced; but associated with this low cost would be a high risk of the project not meeting its completion deadline, since every activity would be critical. Both of these schedules would be unacceptable to management because of their uneven workload and, in one case the very high cost, and in the other the very great risk of not meeting the completion deadline.

Within these two extremes the optimum solution will lie. The activities are now scheduled so that the constraints on the availability of resources are not infringed. Keeping within the resource constraints may result in the time needed to complete the project being extended. If this is so, and the extra time cannot be allowed, some action such as allocating extra resources or deleting inessential activities, will have to be taken. It may also be possible to re-allocate resources, diverting them to critical activities from those that have float time. There may, in fact, be a number of possible solutions to the problem. The important point about PERT and the use of a computer is that because critical activities have been isolated, management knows immediately on what areas of work to concentrate attention, and that since recomputation of schedules is easily achieved on a computer, the effects of all

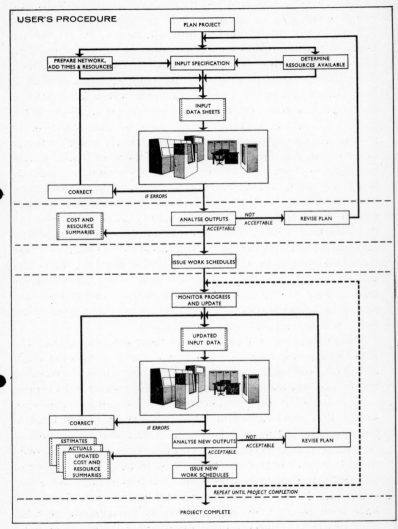

FIG. 33. The total PERT process.

Bar charts can be printed out in various forms to suit individual requirements.

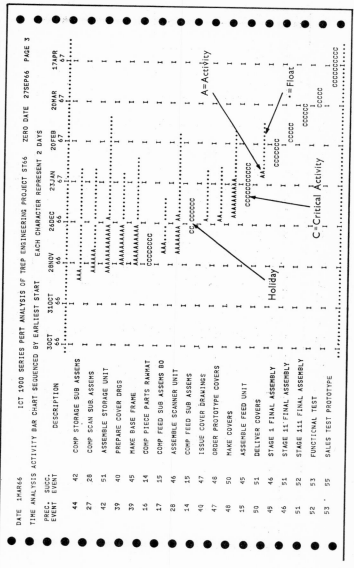

Fig. 34. Activity analysis in bar chart form.

All the activities can be printed to show the information required.

```
DATE 1MAR66        ICT 1900 SERIES PERT ANALYSIS OF TREP ENGINEERING PROJECT ST66        ZERO DATE 1JUN66   PAGE 1
TIME ANALYSIS ACTIVITY REPORT SEQUENCED BY EARLIEST START WITHIN TOTAL FLOAT
```

PREC. EVENT	SUCC. EVENT	DESCRIPTION	REPORT RESP	COST CODE	ACT TIME	EARLIEST START	EARLIEST FINISH	LATEST START	LATEST FINISH	TOTAL FLOAT	FREE FLOAT EARLY/LATE	IND. FLOAT
3	4	PLAN PROTOTYPE	DO		4.0	1JUN66	29JUN66	1JUN66	29JUN66	.	.	*
4	5	ISSUE FEED UNIT SPEC	DO		6.0	29JUN66	10AUG66	29JUN66	10AUG66	.	.	*
5	13	PREP FEED UNIT DRAWINGS	DO		7.3	10AUG66	30CT66	10AUG66	30CT66	.	.	*
13	16	OBT LAST FEED RAW MAT	PUR		8.0	30CT66	28NOV66	30CT66	28NOV66	.	.	*
16	14	COMP PIECE PARTS RAWMAT	PUR		3.0	28NOV66	19DEC66	28NOV66	19DEC66	.	.	*
14	15	COMP FEED SUB ASSEMS	WKS		3.0	19DEC66	11JAN67	19DEC66	11JAN67	.	.	*
15	45	ASSEMBLE FEED UNIT	WKS		4.0	11JAN67	8FEB67	11JAN67	8FEB67	.	.	*
45	46	STAGE 1 FINAL ASSEMBLY	WKS		2.2	8FEB67	24FEB67	8FEB67	24FEB67	.	.	*
46	51	STAGE 11 FINAL ASSEMBLY	KYS		1.3	24FEB67	.8MAR67	24FEB67	8MAR67	.	.	*
51	52	STAGE 111 FINAL ASSEMBLY	WKS		2.0	8MAR67	22MAR67	8MAR67	22MAR67	.	.	*
52	53	FUNCTIONAL TEST	WKS		1.4	22MAR67	4APR67	22MAR67	4APR67	.	.	*
53	55	SALES TEST PROTOTYPE	WKS		4.0	4APR67	2MAY67	4APR67	2MAY67	.	.	*
5	8	ISS 1ST FEED DRGS RAWMAT	DO		1.0	10AUG66	17AUG66	10AUG66	12SEP66	3.3	3.3	3.3
8	16	OBTAIN FEED RAW MATERIAL	PUR		11.0	17AUG66	28NOV66	12SEP66	28NOV66	3.3	3.3	3.3
19	20	ISS 1ST SCAN DRGS P/P	DO		1.0	27JUL66	3AUG66	20SEP66	14NOV66	14.3	3.4	6.4
20	21	MAKE 1ST SCAN P/P	WKS		2.0	30AUG66	13SEP66	14NOV66	4JAN67	15.4	15.4	5.0
21	28	MAKE SCAN SUB ASSEMS	WKS		4.0	13SEP66	6DEC66	4JAN67	1FEB67	15.4	8.0	6.0
38	32	COMPLETE STORAGE PIECE P	WKS		2.0	13SEP66	4NOV66	4JAN67	18JAN67	15.4	5.3	6.2
32	33	ISS 1ST STORAGE UNIT DRG	DO		1.0	20JUL66	27JUL66	27SEP66	17NOV66	16.1	3.2	17.0
4	10	ISSUE TAPE UNIT SPEC	DO		5.0	29JUN66	3AUG66	26OCT66	30NOV66	17.0	.	*
10	18	OBTAIN TAPE UNIT QUOTE	SUB		3.0	3AUG66	24AUG66	30NOV66	21DEC66	17.0	.	*
18	24	OBT APPROVAL TAPE QUOTE	SUB		1.2	24AUG66	2SEP66	21DEC66	3JAN67	17.0	.	*
24	31	ISSUE CONTRACT TAPE UNIT	SUB		1.0	2SEP66	9SEP66	3JAN67	10JAN67	17.0	.	*
31	36	OBTAIN TAPE UNITS	SUB		6.0	9SEP66	21OCT66	10JAN67	21FEB67	17.0	17.0	*
36	46	DELIVER TAPE UNITS	SUB		.3	10OCT66	26OCT66	21FEB67	24FEB67	17.0	17.0	*
33	37	MAKE 1ST STORAGE P/P	WKS		2.2	19AUG66	6SEP66	17NOV66	5JAN67	17.2	7.3	4.3
37	42	MAKE STORAGE SUB ASSEMS	WKS		3.2	6SEP66	22NOV66	9JAN67	1FEB67	17.2		*

(annotation at right: Activities with most Float)

FIG. 35. Activity analysis sequences by earliest start date within total float time.

**Resource
Analysis**
*The availability of company resources at the right time is often the controlling
factor in the successful completion of projects. It is therefore, in many cases, an
integral factor in establishing work schedules.*

*Many forms of resource analyses are available and these can be printed out in
tabular or bar chart form. Histograms can also be printed to show the work load
on any resource.*

The following example shows the forward load in the Assembly Department.

Key
{
 * = *Normal Availability*
 T = *Threshold Availability*
 - = *Utilization*
}

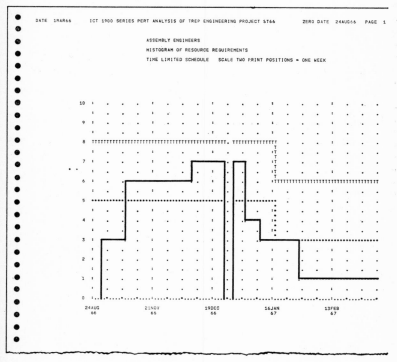

FIG. 36. Resource analysis histogram.

Cost Analysis

An example of one of the forms of cost analysis which is available is shown below. This graphical presentation of financial progress enables management to see at a glance current status and the future trends of project costs.

Key
- X = *Planned Cost*
- A = *Actual Expenditure*
- E = *Revised Estimated Expenditure*
- V = *Value of Work Completed*

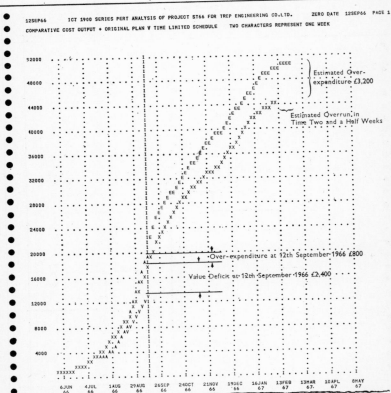

FIG. 37. Cost analysis histogram.

feasible solutions can be seen before any one is selected. This ability to revise schedules rapidly, and simulate the effects of a number of feasible policies, is illustrated in Fig. 33.

Once a suitable plan for the project has been found, the relative time values associated with the project are placed on a calendar basis. It may be, for instance, that the time the project is estimated to take to complete is 200 days. Suppose that the product being launched is particularly pertinent to the Christmas season; it may then be desired to complete the project by the middle of October so that, allowing time for distribution, the product will be available in shops in time for the Christmas market. The start date for the project must therefore be set for 200 days earlier.

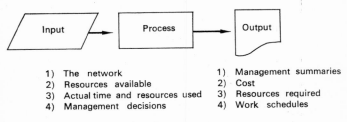

Input	Process	Output

1) The network
2) Resources available
3) Actual time and resources used
4) Management decisions

1) Management summaries
2) Cost
3) Resources required
4) Work schedules

Fig. 38. Progressing the project.

When work has begun, the progress of the project can be controlled using the PERT network and the selected schedule. As data becomes available on the actual cost of activities, and the time and resources used, this can be read into the computer to replace the original estimates and update the schedule. At specified intervals, daily or weekly, reports on the state of the project as regards time, cost, and resources can be printed out to keep management informed (see Figs. 34–37). If the schedule needs adjustment, the effects of various adjustments can be simulated, and the most appropriate action taken. This process is illustrated in Fig. 38.

The question of extending the time taken to complete the project may again arise, but the considerations to be taken into account at this stage are different. Since the work has been started, and the date of the deadline fixed, there arises a cost consideration in the value of sales that will be lost through missing part or all of the Christmas market. There will also be indirect costs, such as if the effectiveness of the publicity campaign is reduced. On the other hand, there may be some reduction in the cost of producing the product associated with the extended

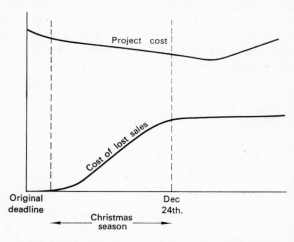

FIG. 39. Cost result of extending project deadline.

schedule. If extra resources are to be allocated in order to meet the scheduled deadline, the cost of these must be weighed against the cost of not meeting the deadline. The cost of lost sales will, in the case of the Christmas product, rise steeply throughout the season and then even out after the end of the season. The cost of the project is likely to drop slightly if the time allowed for it is extended, and then increase as the time extension becomes unduly long. An estimate of the cost in lost sales can be made from sales forecasts, and the saving or cost associated with extending the project can be obtained by simulating the time extension on the PERT network and having a cost analysis printed out. The overall cost picture might be as shown in Fig. 39. The cost of extra resources needed to meet the deadline can then be compared with the probable cost of lost sales through not meeting the deadline and an appropriate decision taken.

Thus PERT is a means of providing management with the detailed information essential to the making of effective decisions. A complex operation is not only difficult to plan and progress, but also usually affords a number of different courses of action out of any crisis that may occur. A decision may have to be taken quickly, however, particularly in markets where conditions change rapidly. The advantage of having detailed information instantly to hand, such information as can be provided using a PERT network processed by computer, is in these circumstances of inestimable value.

CHAPTER 14

Control of Salesmen

THE selling effort of a company can be divided into two categories; personal selling and advertising. The former method of selling is dealt with in this chapter, and the latter method in the following chapter. Controlling both forms of selling is an extremely complex operation, since the nature of many of the factors involved is often peculiar to given companies or products, and the relationships between factors difficult to ascertain and quantify. The examples given in this chapter are simplified for the sale of clarity, but the complications that may arise in practice are indicated in outline.

Personal selling is an expensive business. Good salesmen can command high wages, the expenses that they necessarily incur in their work are considerable, and the effective working day of a salesman is short. Since the cost of employing salesmen is high whatever their quality, the first and most important principle is to ensure that only good salesmen are selected. Although a computer can be of use in monitoring the performance of salesmen, it cannot help in their selection; this is a task for a well-briefed personnel department backed up by a comprehensive training program and on-the-job assessment by experienced members of the sales force. It is because the ability of salesmen is so closely associated with the individual personality that assessment of selling potential is largely intuitive. Since the type of salesman required varies considerably from market to market, generalization about selection procedures is impossible. If, however, some form of questionnaire were used as a part of the selection process, the answers given could be evaluated by computer, in a way analogous to that described in Chapter 9, Credit Control. This would be practical only if the sales force were very large and subject to a considerable turnover in staff.

Where the computer can be of use is in determining the size and distribution of the sales force, and in evaluating its performance. The distribution of the sales force depends on two main factors; the number of visits that the salesman can make in the time allotted to him, and the amount of territory that he must have in order to be able to earn a reasonable wage. The information required involves a knowledge of the current and potential market for a product and much of this information could be available from the market file described in Chapter 10, Market Research. In order to estimate the number of salesmen who should be allocated to a given sales area, some estimate of the effect of different degrees of personal selling is necessary. An experiment such as the following could be tried. The market file could be analysed to provide lists of customers classified according to their estimated sales potential. Salesmen could then be told to spend different amounts of time with each customer over a number of sales periods, and the effect on sales noted. From such an experiment useful information might be obtained on the optimum amount of time that could be spent on each class of customer. Given the amount of time that needs to be spent on each customer, and making allowance for time to be spent seeking new customers, an estimate can be made of the size of sales force needed, and what this will cost.

Supposing that salesmen have been allocated individual areas as their territory, there remains the travelling salesman problem, to which a simplified approach is given below. Each hour that a salesman spends travelling between customers is expensive not only in car usage but also in that he is not selling. Any reduction in this double expense is thus very desirable, and will result in effect in a double saving, diminished travelling expenditure, and more time for selling. The solution to the travelling salesman problem therefore lies in finding the shortest combination of routes between all the customers to be visited. Unfortunately, the solution is not that simple in practice. Early closing days, market days, customer's preferred times for seeing salesmen, urgent calls from customers, and days the salesman has to spend away from his territory for conferences or briefing, are just some of the factors that serve to complicate the situation. Nevertheless, many of these complications can be accommodated in standard computer software.

The travelling salesman problem is in essence similar to the type of problem known as vehicle scheduling, the principal basic difference being that in the latter type of problem allowance has to be made for the load-carrying capacity of vehicles. The standard approach to the problem is based on linear programming. The constraints which may be specified include a time limit for each route, which could be a working day or week, and times at which visits may not be made; thus allowance can be made for early closing days and customers' preferred times for seeing salesmen. Other data to be input includes the towns to be visited, the position of each town based on the National Grid map reference, and an assumed average speed for the salesman. Constants can be set to allow for city traffic conditions, and the time spent with each customer, and the time spent visiting various customers in one town can similarly be allowed for.

It is assumed that the routes must pass through a common point, which could be the sales area office or the salesman's home. The program first calculates the distances between the various towns, and between the towns and the central point, say the sales office. These distances will be "as the crow flies", and are converted to road distances by adjustment with a constant. A fictitious initial solution is assumed, and the program then modifies this if any improvement can be made within the restrictions imposed by the constraints. The process can be represented diagrammatically as in Fig. 40. Suppose that the routes at one stage in the program are as on the left-hand side of the figure. The program might eliminate the distances AE and AD by adding the journey from E to D. The saving in distance would thus be $AE + AD - ED$. If this adjustment violated the specified constraints it could not be allowed, of course, and the program would try other adjustments. The process is repeated until no further improvements can be made, and the solution is then printed out. The towns are listed in the order in which they are to be visited along the route, and the time spent on the road and with

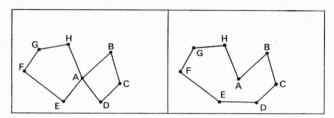

FIG. 40. Finding the shortest route.

customers is listed for each town, together with the overall totals. An example of a computer printout is given in Fig. 41.

Many companies have managed to save thousands of pounds in salesmen's expenses by using such methods of controlling salesmen's movements. The extra benefit of allowing salesmen more time with customers should also produce a gain to the company concerned, so that even relatively unsophisticated attempts to solve the travelling salesman problem can produce very significant financial results.

If selling is to be really successful, close control of the salesmen's performance is imperative; this control has several purposes. One is to allow an evaluation of the salesmen's individual performance, another is to assess the effectiveness of the incentives given to salesmen, and yet another to provide information on the adequacy of territory allocation. It can be appreciated that since any market is in a dynamic state, territory allocation should be subject to constant scrutiny and will sometimes need revision. Before any rational attempt can be made to control salesmen's performance, however, the objectives of selling must be defined in order to provide a standard for judgement.

In general, the objective of selling is to obtain a profit, and yet it is surprising how often salesmen are judged on some other criterion. Salesmen are frequently judged, for instance, on the volume of sales they obtain; and yet the volume of sales may bear no set relationship to the profit obtained from them. A more logical basis on which to evaluate a salesman's performance would be his contribution to profit, or, as an approximation of this, the gross profit obtained from the sales that he makes. This means that the salesman must know the relative profitability of the products that he sells, and will encourage him to discriminate in

ROUTE 6

REL INDEX	DELIVERY POINT	MASTER INDEX	ROAD TIME HRS MNS		TOWN TIME HRS MNS		RUNNING TOTAL HRS MNS	
11	KEMPSTON	11	1	14	0	08	1	22
34	KIMBOLTON	34	0	41	0	14	2	17
32	SPALDWICK	32	0	15	0	07	2	39
38	ST IVES	38	0	38	0	53	4	10
53	PAPWORTH EVERARD	53	0	22	0	08	4	40
40	ELTISLEY	40	0	11	0	07	4	58
39	ST NEOTS	39	0	21	0	07	5	26
19	MAULDEN	19	0	49	0	16	6	31
18	AMPTHILL	18	0	09	0	09	6	49
16	FLITWICK	16	0	09	0	19	7	17
0	AYLESBURY	0	0	58	0	00	8	15

ROUTE SUMMARY

TOTAL NUMBER OF DROPS—	16
TOTAL TRAVELLING TIME —	5-47
TOTAL DROP TIME—	2-28
TOTAL ROUTE TIME—	8-15

Fig. 41. Computer printout of solution.

his selling in favour of the products which produce the greatest profit for his company. Provided that products are properly costed, the relative profitability of each should not be difficult to gauge. Another factor to be taken into account in assessing a salesman is the contribution to long-term sales which he makes by calling on potential customers. If this part of his work is not considered, the tendency will be to work the existing market to death and ignore the potential customer, with disastrous long-term consequences. A form of extra bonus for sales to new customers would be one way of providing the necessary incentive.

The establishment of incentives is a complex business, involving an appreciation of what motivates salesmen. Any good salesman must achieve some satisfaction from the mere act of selling, but other inducements must usually also be offered. The most usual, of course, is money, but even this is difficult to administrate. In some markets, selling is done by individual salesmen, in others by groups; the provision of incentives for individuals in what is essentially a group operation could serve to harm the selling effort. Sometimes incentives are based on a comparison between current and preceding periods' or years' figures; while this has some advantages, it means that a salesman having an extremely good year can be severely penalized for it in subsequent years. These are just some of the traps inherent in establishing incentives.

A general basis for establishing incentives is to calculate a sales quota for each salesman. The sales quota should not be confused with either the expected sales or the potential sales. The sales quota should be the target to which a given salesman will react most effectively, taking into account the salesman's personality and the nature of his territory. Some salesmen strive most for a target they can never meet, while others become discouraged in these circumstances, and will work more effectively given a quota that they can invariably beat. In such a variable quota system, three salesmen working in similar territories might earn similar amounts, the one by exceeding his quota by a third, another by achieving his quota exactly, and the last by failing to meet his quota by a third.

The administration of a control system involving so many variables would be extremely difficult by manual methods. Moreover, the constant necessity to adjust the value of the variables, so that salesmen are not penalized for past performances, or do not find themselves in exhausted territories, means that the system would be virtually impossible to work without the aid of a computer. Given a computer, however, the control operation could be achieved relatively simply by establishing a salesman's file. A salesman's file could include such information as personal details of each salesman, his quota, and associated commission; his grade of territory, according to existing and potential customers could also be included, and details of his past performance summarized by sales period, with a record of sales by product within customer type, and the associated contribution to gross profit.

The file could be updated using survey data obtained for the market file described in Chapter 10, Market Research, and by selling reports submitted by the salesmen. Selling reports should be designed to show only relevant information, such as the customers visited, orders obtained, new contacts made, and so on; it is both tedious for salesmen and useless to management to include narrative on sales reports which adds up to a simple "no comment". Although the salesman's file will need to be kept up to date, there is no reason why the routine activities recorded on it should concern management. The sales manager will have his own estimate of the performance that should be achieved by each salesman. A relationship can be established between the performance management expects and the sales quota allotted to each salesman, and this relationship, given a numerical value, can be inserted in each salesman's record as a control parameter. A salesman's record would then be printed out for management attention only when the salesman's performance was significantly different from management's expectations. In such a case, the sales manager would have immediately available a detailed record of the salesman's past and current performance to indicate what action should be taken. The salesmen's file would provide not only close control and flexibility in the control of the sales force, but also information which could be of use in the selection of salesmen.

CHAPTER 15

Control of Advertising

THE difficulties associated with the control of advertising are many and extreme, so that this account will confine itself to an outline of the problem and possible solutions. The difficulties arise from the lack of detailed and definite information on the effects of advertising, and from the multiplicity of factors that influence buying. It is not possible to assess the effect of an advertising campaign accurately unless all other influences on the market can be evaluated so that they can be quantified.

The first information the sales manager needs to have is the relationship between advertising expenditure and increased profit. The sole justification for advertising is evidently the increased profit it will produce; depending on his advertising budget, the sales manager will want to know either the lowest advertising cost that will achieve a given profit goal, or else the optimum point between advertising cost and profit that will maximize profit. Supposing that the latter case is true, the information could theoretically be obtained by plotting on a graph the relationship between sales revenue and advertising cost. This is shown as the line A/S in Fig. 42. It is reasonable to suppose that some sales would be obtained without any advertising; a little advertising will have a little impact, and a large campaign a big impact, until eventually the saturation point is approached and diminishing returns set in. It can be seen that the optimum sales/advertising relationship will lie somewhere along the part of the line A/S between the point where the ratio of sales to unit cost in advertising begins to increase significantly and the point where diminishing returns are first encountered. In order to plot the actual point of optimacy, a line *SR* representing sales revenue is drawn, and where a line parallel to *SR* meets the upper curve of *AS* at a tangent is the optimum point *Y*. A line parallel to *SR* meeting the lower curve of *AS* at a tangent would fix the point of minimum profit. The distance *YZ* represents the difference between advertising cost and sales revenue at the optimum point.

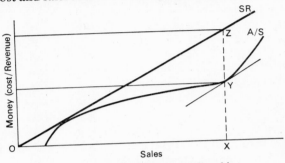

FIG. 42. Sales/advertising relationship.

Although this method of establishing the optimum level of advertising is valid in principle, the problem has been simplified. For instance, it is assumed that the sales/advertising relationship is known. In practice the precise effect of advertising on sales is difficult to establish, and so the effects of advertising are inferred from estimates of the size and type of audience being reached, and the reactions of the audience. One of the problems, particularly with expensive products, is that there is often a considerable lapse in time between advertisements being seen and any resultant purchases being made. A person may be tempted to buy an ice cream on the spur of the moment, but the capital outlay involved in buying a car will cause the same person to react less hastily; he may, for example, need time to accumulate the necessary money.

An important factor influencing the effect of advertising issued by one company, is the amount of advertising issued by other companies in the same market. Some recent research suggests the conclusions shown in Table 8. It would appear that any advertisements for product A publicize not only this product but also this type of product. Therefore, a slight decrease in the level of advertising by competitors will cause sales of product A to increase; a slight increase in the level of competitors' advertising will have the reverse effect. A large decrease in the level of competitors' advertising, however, causes public attention to be withdrawn from the type of product; product A's share of the market may increase, but the number of sales will decrease because the market will have shrunk.

TABLE 8. RELATIONSHIP BETWEEN ADVERTISING FOR PRODUCT A AND ADVERTISING FOR COMPETITIVE PRODUCTS

Advertising level for		Sales of product A
Product A	Competitive products	
Constant	Small decrease	Increase
Constant	Small increase	Decrease
Constant	Large decrease	Decrease

Computers have not so far been widely used in the control of advertising because of the difficulty, as was stated earlier, of discovering relationships such as those described above between factors influencing the market, and in particular because of the difficulty of quantifying these relationships. However, two examples of ways in which computers have been used successfully to control aspects of advertising are described below.

Given a certain budget with which to advertise product A, the sales manager wishes to know how best to spend this on the various advertising media available in order to reach the largest and most receptive audience. The types of potential customer can be ascertained either from the market file, or possibly by means of a market research survey. Suitable media for advertising the product can then be selected; information on the type and size of audience reached by various magazines and newspapers, television, radio, and films, is readily available, and the number of potential customers reached per unit expenditure on advertising can be calculated. This data can be held on magnetic tape, or some other suitable form of storage, a quantitative value being assigned to each medium for every class of potential customer. Allowance can be made for variations in the size of audience reached by successive advertisements in the same medium; for instance, the second time an advertisement is inserted in a newspaper, the total audience reached will be greater than, but not double, the audience reached by the first insertion. The problem of media selection, admittedly somewhat simplified, is then one of selecting the optimum combination of media that will reach the largest suitable audience within the constraint imposed by the size of the advertising budget. The problem can be resolved using standard linear programming routines on the computer. The value of a computer can be seen in that if there are only four suitable media for advertising a product, there is a choice of fifteen possible combinations without even considering the relative importance to be given to each medium in any combination. There may well be ten or more suitable media from which to choose an optimum combination, in which case a solution to the problem could hardly be attempted by manual methods.

A more complex use of the computer in advertising control involves the creation of a model to simulate the market to be studied. The model is created to reflect the brand switching that will occur with variations in the level of advertising. The complexity of this method of control derives from the necessity to hold constant all other factors influencing the market, such as share of the market and other promotional activities, so that the effects of advertising alone can be studied. In order to hold these factors constant, they must be quantified, and as was indicated at the beginning of this section, the effort involved is considerable. This form of control would be most feasible in a steady market.

PART IV

More Complex Uses of the Computer

CHAPTER 16

Management Games

MANAGEMENT games are a comparatively recent development in the field of scientific techniques, but have been increasingly widely used in the past few years. They derive from the theory of games, which in the commercial context is concerned with the behaviour of companies in a competitive environment; more precisely, the behaviour of one company is usually studied in relation to that of competing companies. The behaviour of a company in competition with a natural environment may also be studied in a similar way. The purpose of the theory of games is to enable various possible company policies to be evaluated so that the most appropriate one can be selected to be put into effect. The policies which each of the companies competing in a market can adopt are established, and the results of each policy being adopted are estimated. It is assumed that each competing company will select the policy which should prove most profitable to itself, and the gain for each company can then be estimated. According to the results achieved by the policy adopted in one period, each company will adapt its policy during the next period in order to try to secure a more favourable position. Thus the policy of each company is to some extent influenced by the policies of the other companies competing in the same market. When a company is competing against its natural environment, on the other hand, there is clearly no question of the natural environment adapting itself because of policies followed by the company. In this case, instead of other companies' policies being taken into account, statistical data gleaned from observation of natural phenomena is considered. Thus, if the weather is a factor affecting company policy, the policy will be determined taking into consideration the statistical probability of certain weather conditions prevailing at a given time.

These are the principles on which the theory of games is based. The theory has found many applications in determining policies, particularly in assessing the optimum level of bids in submitting tenders for contracts or in purchasing. It has also led to the development of management games for the training of executives. Management games involve creating a model of part of a commercial environment; teams of executives representing companies, are given information regarding their companies and invited to make policy decisions in order to achieve some company objective. The decisions of each team are evaluated against the model, and the results given to the team members; new decisions are then made, and the whole process repeated a predetermined number of times. As the game progresses, the teams begin to appreciate the effects that their decisions are having on their company, and they also gain information about the environment in which they are competing, and the policies of competing companies and their effects. One of the advantages to be gained from this sort of training is that executives learn to think in terms of the whole company. The necessity for taking decisions in the context of the whole company, rather than in terms of an individual department or division, has already been stressed in this book. Nevertheless, since executives commonly work in one particular division of a company, the overall perspective is often difficult to appreciate. Management games, by allowing executives to represent the whole company, enable them to see the relationship between the various divisions, and to see how a decision taken in one division can affect other divisions of the same company. Moreover, since the effects of decisions over a period of years can be simulated in a game lasting possibly only a day, executives can be made to see the long-term effects of their decisions and to work with them, the mistakes as well as the successes. Finally, if any executive is not convinced of the advantages to be obtained from scientific management techniques, he has the chance to see the results obtained by their use and, if he wishes, to try to better these results by intuitive means. Simulated bankruptcy, followed perhaps by a tape recording of proceedings in a bankruptcy court, forms a very convincing argument.

If a game is to be of any use in training it must produce results similar to those that would be obtained from a given set of decisions in a given environment in real life. Moreover, the result of a game must depend on the players' skill and judgement and not on anything as arbitrary as luck. These requirements mean that in order to be useful, the model of the environment in a game will be somewhat complex. It is possible to use management games without the aid of a computer, but in order to keep calculation within reasonable limits the computation of results and the refinements permissible in making decisions will in these circumstances necessarily be rather lacking in sophistication. In general, a computer is used to allow for a sophisticated model of the situation, and a panel of judges is present to manipulate the model so that market conditions can be modified, perhaps to simulate a slump or a boom.

The following example of a relatively simple management game illustrates the principles and worth of this form of management training. This game is for three teams of between three and five people, each team representing a different company; it is recommended that each member of the team be allocated a specific role, such as marketing director, financial controller, or managing director. The three companies compete in four marketing areas, each company having a "home" area in which it starts with an advantage, and one area being "foreign" to all companies. A mathematical model simulates the interaction of individual companies' decisions, and calculates each company's share of the market according to the selling price of the product and expenditure on research and development and marketing.

At the start of the game, each company receives a report recording its position at the end of a financial year; all companies start in a similar position. On the basis of this report, each company must make decisions for the next quarter in order to maximize its ratio of net income to total assets or to achieve its planned objective. The decisions to be made cover a fairly wide area in order to give participants experience in corporate decision making. A selling price for the marketed product, and marketing expenditure must be fixed for each of the four areas. Details of production expenditure, research and development expenditure, and plant investment must be given, and an allowance made for transport costs. The total expenditure obviously cannot exceed the cash available to the company. When decisions have been made on cash allocation, this information is entered on a form such as the one shown in Fig. 43 and then punched into a card and input to the computer. A limit is fixed on the time which the companies have to make their decisions.

The computer prints out a report for each of the companies, giving the information shown in Fig. 44. On the basis of this report each company makes its decisions for the following quarter. The companies can assess their performance, and deduce information about the market conditions prevailing in each of the areas. The relative effectiveness of decisions is evaluated in the model by means of constants which can be manipulated by the panel of judges. Modification of the constants modifies market conditions, and this is done gradually so that each company has the chance to notice the change in the market and react accordingly. If companies make serious errors, such as overmarketing their product in one area, they incur a penalty which affects their future performance in that area. If companies wish to make extra cash available, they can sell plant at a price agreed with the judges; this will, of course, affect their production capacity for succeeding quarters. At the end of each financial year a public statement is made of the companies' finances, so that each company can see how the others are progressing. A yearly report is given in Fig. 45.

The game continues for a predetermined number of quarters, the winning company being the one with the highest ratio of net income to total assets; some other criterion could be applied if this was desired. After the game has finished, the judges and teams get together for a post mortem. The teams can be given a chance to

BUSINESS MANAGEMENT EXERCISE

DECISION FORM

CARD COLUMNS		Description
1		Company Number
2 – 3		Period
4 – 5		Price area 1 in £'s (Maximum: £99)
6 – 7		Price area 2 in £'s (Maximum: £99)
8 – 9		Price area 3 in £'s (Maximum: £99)
10 – 11		Price area 4 in £'s (Maximum: £99)
12 – 15	0	1) Marketing area 1 in £1000's (Maximum: £300,000)
16 – 19	0	2) Marketing area 2 in £1000's (Maximum: £300,000)
20 – 23	0	3) Marketing area 3 in £1000's (Maximum: £300,000)
24 – 27	0	4) Marketing area 4 in £1000's (Maximum: £300,000)
28 – 32	0	a) Marketing total in £1000's (Areas 1 – 2 – 3 – 4)
33 – 38	0	b) Production in £1000's (see note below)
39 – 44	0 0 0	c) Research and development in £1000's (Maximum: £300,000)
45 – 50	0	d) Plant investment in £1000's
51 – 56	0	e) Allowance for transport in £1000's
Not Punched		Total cash allocation in £1000's (a – b – c – d – e)
57 – 62		Cash available in £1000's as shown in report.

N.B. (1) Production allocation must not be below £2,000,000 or above cost of producing at plant capacity.

(2) Total allocation must not exceed cash available.

FIG. 43. Business management exercise decision form.

BUSINESS MANAGEMENT EXERCISE – MANAGEMENT REPORT

	Company 1	Period 0	Information		Total
	1	Area Market 2	3	4	813000
Orders Received	158000	158000	158000	339000	813000
Sales	158000	158000	158000	339000	813000
Marketing Exp.	350000	350000	350000	750000	1800000

Your Company Area Sales Analysis

	1	2	3	4	Total
Orders Received	112000	23000	23000	113000	271000
Sales	112000	23000	23000	113000	271000
Marketing Exp.	250000	50000	50000	250000	600000
Sales Income	4480000	920000	920000	4520000	10840000
Delivered Unit Cost	35.00	37.00	37.00	36.00	

Your Company Production Reports and Estimates

	10% Less Current 227000	Current 252000	10% More 277000	Plant Capacity 260000	Inventory 17000
Quantity	227000	252000	277000	260000	17000
Unit Cost	35.91	35.12	34.40	34.85	33.84
Total Cost	8152000	8850000	9529000	9079000	575000

%Change		Income Statement
Your Company		
Sales Income		10840000.
Cost of Goods Sold		9493000
Transport		205000
Marketing Exp.		600000
Research and Dev.		100000
Depreciation		104000
Income Before Tax		338000
Taxes		169000
Net Income		169000
Cash Available		10362000

Fig. 44. Business management exercise management report.

		Assets	Change	% Change
	Cash	11044200	357600	3
	Inventory	NIL	NIL	NIL
Company 1	Plant Invest.	6121500	283200	4
	Total Assets	17165800	640900	3
	Cash	11585100	702400	6
	Inventory	NIL	NIL	NIL
Company 2	Plant Invest.	5603400	114400	2—
	Total Assets	17188500	588000	3
	Cash	11951500	2683900	28
	Inventory	NIL	2314700	100—
Company 3	Plant Invest.	5587400	96700	1—
	Total Assets	17538900	272500	1

		Area 1	Area 2	Area 3	Area 4	
	Price	41.00	42.00	44.00	41.00	
Company 1						Total Sales 281600
						Net Income 641500
	Price	42.00	42.00	45.00	42.00	
Company 2						Total Sales 285800
						Net Income 588700
	Price	45.00	45.00	50.00	45.00	
Company 3						Total Sales 265200
						Net Income 273100

FIG. 45. Business management exercise yearly statement.

explain their policies and why they were adopted, and the judges, who could be experienced marketing men, can explain why various policies had the effects that they did and where companies made errors. The value of a game such as the one described is that it is sufficiently uncomplicated to be useful for teaching purposes, while at the same time it is sufficiently realistic to underline its point, namely, the need to integrate diverse company functions.

More complicated games have been devised involving more complex models. The aspects of a company's work covered in the game described above could be dealt with in more detail. Marketing expenditure, for instance, could be subdivided so that decisions would have to be made on the proportion of the total marketing budget to be allocated to advertising and personal selling. Details of the number and distribution of salesmen could also be required, and information on areas of the market could be made obtainable for a certain fee. The specification of production expenditure is capable of amplification in the same way. If desired, allowance could be made for more companies to compete. Executives taking part could also be required to produce calculations, graphs, and charts to justify the decisions that they make, and this material could be inspected by the panel of judges and criticized in the post mortem. Evidently, the more complicated the game, the more complex would need to be the mathematical model used to simulate the market and compute the effects of each company's decisions.

Management games need not necessarily involve more than one company. A company may create a model of itself so that executives in one division can try various policies and simulate their effects on other divisions in the company. In this way executives can gain a deeper appreciation of how their own company works and how their decisions are affecting other divisions. In order to do this, the company would have to create its own model, since the standard models provided for management games by computer manufacturers would be unlikely to reflect accurately enough the operation of any one company in its own particular environment. A model of a specific company need not be limited in its use to educational purposes, however; within the degree of accuracy with which the model reflected the true situation, it could be used for simulating the effects of policy decisions under actual consideration, and could thus be of use for planning marketing policy.

CHAPTER 17

Constructing a Marketing Model

Two terms with which the modern manager should be familiar are "cybernetics" and "industrial dynamics". The former term is given to studies which attempt to discover means of stabilizing systems; cybernetics has a wide variety of applications, mainly outside commerce, but some of its principles, such as the need to establish a signal through feedback to correct conditions of imbalance, are highly pertinent to commercial situations. Industrial dynamics involves the creation of a model of a company in order to study the interaction of the various divisions making up the company. Since both of these terms are frequently used in discussions on simulation, it is better that the manager should be aware of their significance; the context in which they are used can be seen in the ensuing description of the creation and use of a marketing model.

The creation of models to be used for simulation purposes is almost invariably a complex operation, since one of the principal reasons that simulation is used is that the process to be studied is so complicated as to defy analysis, and hence the use of simulation techniques. Nevertheless, it is possible to create a simple model in order to demonstrate the principles involved, and to indicate ways in which the model can be developed.

Suppose that a given company wishes to stabilize demand for its product. Demand for the product is fluctuating to such an extent that the company is frequently in the position of either being unable to meet all the orders it receives or else holding large quantities of stock and having to slow down production. It is therefore decided to create a model of the company's principal operations in order to try to discover the factors affecting this situation and see if they can be controlled so that demand can be stabilized. A most important consideration in any forecasting system is the time factor; the time cycles in the company's operations must therefore be established by observation. It is necessary to know, for instance, how long it takes for an order to be satisfied from stock, or how long if the order has to go through production. It is also necessary to know how long an advertising campaign takes to launch, and how long to take effect. Assuming that this company allocates its advertising budget for one period as a fixed percentage

FIG. 46. Advertising/orders time cycle.

of sales income in the previous period, the time cycle for orders and advertising might be as illustrated in Fig. 46. If the market research takes 1 month, the advertising campaign 2 months to plan and launch, and the effect of the campaign on orders is not noticed for a further month, then the significant cycle time is 4 months. This is an important item of information for production scheduling. The time relationships for all the activities to be included in the model are ascertained; the time scales in the production and loading and delivery processes could also be included. It is sometimes possible to establish a cycle in customers purchasing. If, for instance, equipment is being sold, it is possible to estimate the life of the equipment and hence when it will need to be replaced; when the equipment begins to wear out, every past customer of the same period becomes a potential new customer again. With just a time model management may gain a lot of useful information; by varying times, accelerating or slowing down production, or delivery, for instance, and simulating the effect that this has on the market, ideas for future policies may emerge. In the colour photography industry, variations in the time taken to return customers' colour slides after processing has little effect unless the time taken drops to a week or below. At this point, there is a very significant sales increase. The reason for this sales

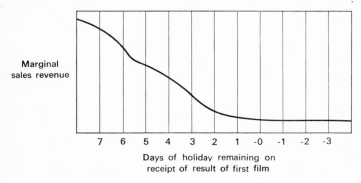

FIG. 47. Variation of marginal sales with delay in return of first film.

increase is that people most frequently take a fortnight's summer holiday; many people are using colour film for the first time, and therefore wish to see the resultant slides of their first film before buying a second. If a customer receives the slides from his first film while still on holiday, and the slides are satisfactory, he is very likely to buy another film; once his holiday is over, however, he is less likely to buy another film for some time. This situation is illustrated in Fig. 47. If the customer receives the slides from his first film while he still has almost a week of holiday remaining, he may well buy two more films; with only 3 days' holiday left he is more likely to buy just one more film. The usefulness of information on customers' purchasing habits is clear; the implications of the above information on the time taken to process colour slides, and on the stocks of film that should be held are extremely important.

Apart from the time relationships network, networks covering the flow of money, materials, manpower, and information will also usually be included. The relationship between sales income and the advertising budget, for instance, would be included, and the relationship between advertising expenditure and sales income. These two relationships may provide a clue to the reasons for the previously mentioned company's sales fluctuation problem, as will be seen.

One common cause of fluctuation in any company's sales is that slight but general variations in retail selling are magnified at the manufacturing end of the process. If a retailer sells less of a product during one period than during a previous period, he will be holding larger stocks and will therefore need to re-order less in order to maintain his usual stock level. He may also conclude that the sales trend is downwards, and will therefore decide to reduce his stock level. Thus the effect of decreased sales in one period can be magnified in the next period's order figures. This process can act in reverse when sales rise from one period to the next.

As stated earlier, the company with the sales fluctuation problem allocated its advertising budget as a fixed proportion of sales income from the previous period, say 3%. Given that 4 months elapse between the fixing of the advertising budget and the time that the effects of the resultant campaign are felt, and that 1 month elapses between the time this money is spent and the result on sales seen, the marketing model is constructed including the following equations:

Sales income = Advertising expenditure one month ago × ratio of advertising expenditure to sales

Advertising expenditure one month ago = Sales income four months ago × 3%

The result of tying advertising expenditure to sales income can now be seen. It can be assumed that this policy was decided on in a period of economic stability. If a slump then occurs, the market hardens causing the stable advertising expenditure to produce less sales; the reduction in sales causes a reduction in sales income, which in turn causes a reduction in advertising expenditure. The reduction in advertising expenditure causes sales to decrease still further and a spiral is entered that can only be broken by a change in external economic conditions. A boom period would produce a spiral in the opposite direction. Thus, this marketing policy not only fails to help the company adjust to uncontrollable fluctuations in external market conditions, but actually magnifies the effect of these conditions on the company. By its policy, the company is therefore contributing to its own instability. An apparently more logical policy would be to reduce advertising expenditure in proportion to the increase in sales. Alternatively, some sales target could be set, and advertising expenditure adjusted to achieve this target. The most suitable policy to follow will depend on factors peculiar to the company concerned.

The above example illustrates the principles of the construction and use of a marketing model, but has greatly simplified the process. Only advertising expenditure was considered in finding a solution to the company's problem, and this is very unlikely to be the case in practice. It would be a mistake to suppose that marketing problems can be solved merely by manipulating advertising expenditure. Moreover, even this factor has been considered in simplified form; no allowance was made, for instance, for the relationship mentioned in Chapter 15, Control of Advertising, between the advertising expenditure of one company and that of other companies competing in the same market. For a model to reflect a company's operations accurately, a large number of factors have to be taken into account; it is the consequently considerable amount of calculation involved that requires the use of a computer. The user can thus create models to any degree of complexity that suits his purpose in the knowledge that the necessary calculations will be performed rapidly and accurately. It should always be remembered, however, that the simulated results of policies will be accurate only to the degree that the model has been constructed to represent the real situation.

CHAPTER 18

Real Time Processing of Orders

THE meaning of "real-time" has changed considerably since the term was first coined. The origin of the term lies with the development of guided missiles. It can be appreciated that when situations are simulated on a computer, there is a time scale inherent in the changes in the simulation model. When the situation being simulated for study changes very rapidly in real life, it is sometimes desirable to slow down the simulation of the situation, so that the time scale of the simulation to the real situation might be, for instance, 10 : 1. Similarly, in different circumstances it might be desirable to accelerate the situation on the simulation model; an example of this appears in Chapter 16, Management Games, where the effect of companies' policies on a market over a period of years is simulated during a day or two. Sometimes, such as when testing control systems, it is necessary to simulate situations using a time scale factor of unity, simulated time being the same as real time. Thus if the time scale is 1 : 1, the process is said to be conducted in real time.

The number of situations in which it is necessary to work in real time in the strict sense of the term is very limited. The meaning of the term has therefore been extended to include situations in which the delay between a computer receiving data and the response to that data is insignificant. This definition is necessarily relative since in the current generalized use of the term, real time can have different meanings in different circumstances; the concept will become clearer as it is illustrated. As real time systems have developed, so has the use of direct access devices. It can be appreciated that if a request for information is input to the computer, and the response time is to be insignificant, it must be possible to access items of information in a random manner. If a file of records had to be searched sequentially to find any particular record, then the average time taken to find a record would no longer be insignificant. A distinction can now be made to elucidate the nature of real time processing. A contrast is sometimes made between real time and batch processing. Files are usually updated by means of batch processing; since there may be a large number of transactions affecting say, a customer accounts file, in a short space of time, little is to be gained by updating the file each time that a transaction occurs. Instead, batches of transactions are assembled, sorted to the same sequence as the file, and the file is updated at convenient intervals with the batch of transactions that have occurred since the previous updating run. Since the delay in collecting and assembling a batch of transactions would infringe on even the most general definition of real time processing, however, a feature of real time processing is that transactions are dealt with individually as they occur.

There are several advantages to be gained from real time processing, as will be seen in the example outlined below. Associated with these advantages, however, is the higher cost of the necessary hardware and associated programming effort. As has already been stated, direct access devices must be used instead of the cheaper magnetic tape; typewriter terminals would also be needed to request or receive random information from the files stored on the direct access devices. In many circumstances this extra cost can easily be justified.

The first examples of real time processing of orders were provided in airline booking systems. Under the manual system, orders received at the central office had to be matched against lists of flights and seats available. The volume of paper work can be appreciated considering that BEA, for instance, carries several million passengers per year to some seventy destinations. There is, moreover, a need for great flexibility, since passengers may change their flights, or flights may have to be rescheduled at the last minute because of delays caused by bad weather or other reasons.

Yet services have to be maintained with the minimum of aircraft and crews if the company is to remain solvent. The matching of aircraft and crews to flights therefore calls for very tight scheduling. The manual system is not only slow, but also highly prone to errors of transcription. When a customer requested a ticket, a passenger record card would have to be made out showing details of his itinerary, and insertions made on passenger check lists for every flight involved in the journey. If the customer then altered his itinerary in any way, a new passenger record would have to be made out, the relevant insertions made previously on passenger check lists would have to be deleted, and new insertions made. In these circumstances errors of transcription are inevitable, and yet they can cause a great deal of inconvenience and expense. Moreover, in order to avoid over-booking of flights, flights have to be declared fully booked when there are in fact a few seats remaining in order to allow for requests for seats that might be already "in the pipeline".

Under the real time computer system it is possible to reduce considerably the time needed to process an order. A file of flights giving details of the number of seats booked and available, and the names of passengers for each flight can be held on a direct access device; a file of passenger records can be similarly kept. When a request for a seat on a given flight is received at the central office, the file is interrogated to see if the seat is available by typing in the request on a typewriter terminal. If a seat is available, it is deleted from the flight record, and a passenger record is typed in to be stored in the passenger record file. If a customer wishes to change his flight, his record can be retrieved from the file within two or three seconds, and his record can be adjusted and flight records updated in a matter of a few more seconds. Should erroneous data be typed in, such as booking a seat on a flight which is already fully booked, an error message will be automatically typed out by the typewriter terminal to bring the error immediately to the attention of the booking clerk. Errors of flight number, date, or destination would be treated in the same way, so that errors of transcription are virtually eliminated. Moreover, since the real time system is so much faster than the manual system, there is no longer any need to classify flights as fully booked until all seats have been taken; allowance for orders that may be "in the pipeline" is no longer necessary, and so there is no risk of aircraft leaving with empty seats because assumed orders did not in fact materialize, or of customers being disappointed because of insufficient allowance being made for orders "in the pipeline". Other advantages are gained by holding details of aircraft and crews in computer files; greater flexibility is obtained by being able to reschedule flights, aircraft, and crews at electronic speeds. Finally, since the paper work which has to be performed by sales and booking staff is considerably reduced, they can concentrate on the part of their work in which human relations are most important, their contact with the public.

There is obvious scope for similar real time systems in organizations which deal with a large number of bookings which have to be satisfied quickly, and where the state of facilities needs to be known with up-to-the-minute accuracy. Hotel accommodation and entertainment booking could benefit from the use of real time systems. The feasibility of real time systems is not limited to such applications, however; analogous "booking" situations can often be found in commerce generally. There is no difference in essence between passengers reserving seats from a central pool of flights and orders for any product being satisfied from a central pool of products. If large volumes of orders have to be satisfied in a short space of time, involving a great deal of paper work, then the same benefits may accrue to a manufacturing organization from the use of a real time system as accrue to airlines.

Suppose that a company manufactures and markets one basic product in a number of different forms, sizes, colours, and so on. If the volume of trade is sufficiently large, involving satisfying possibly 5000 or more orders a day, then the company could benefit from a real time system as described below. Orders received by the company are punched into cards and stored on to a magnetic disc in batches at convenient intervals; this can be done every day, week, or month, according to how soon on average the orders are to be satisfied. The provision of a typewriter terminal in the receiving department allows urgent new orders to be typed directly into store; last minute alterations to orders already stored on disc can be made in the same way. Another typewriter terminal is provided in the dispatch department. As packages of the manufactured product arrive at dispatch from production, details of the quantity, type, colour, etc., of the product contained in the package are typed in on the typewriter terminal. This data is compared to orders held on disc, and the package allocated to an appropriate order; the order is deleted, and a label printed out by the typewriter giving all necessary details such as the contents of the package and the customer's name and address. The real time system thus provides flexibility in the receipt and scheduling of orders and speed in dispatching them.

The system described in outline above could be developed into a more comprehensive and sophisticated system. If details of the availability of each variation on the basic product are held on disc, customers' inquiries can be dealt with in real time. Customers' inquiries can be telephoned from sales offices to the central receipt department, and the availability file interrogated by means of the typewriter terminal. In this way customers could be informed immediately as to when they could expect delivery of their order or alternatively what range of orders could be supplied by a given date. Such a system would necessitate the availability file being updated from inventory and production data at very frequent intervals, possibly even in real time. The system can also be developed to compute loading and delivery schedules.

CHAPTER 19

Data Transmission

THE advantages of real time processing have already been described with reference to airline reservation systems. It will be remembered that certain benefits accrued from booking clerks at the central office being able, on receipt of a booking request, to interrogate passenger and flight files held on a magnetic disc store. The transmission of orders from sales offices to the central office was not considered and yet, given real time working at the central office, the transmission of orders to the central office will be the longest part of the whole ordering process. Orders may be transmitted by post, telephone, or telegram, and while these means are cheap, they can also be relatively slow and a source of error. The more intermediaries there are between the customer and the placing of his order, the greater the chance of errors occurring. It would therefore be better if the central computer files could be interrogated directly from distant sales offices, by means of data transmission systems.

Data transmission in association with the use of data processing is not a new practice; for many years data has been transmitted over telegraph wires between punched-card and paper-tape installations. The concepts and reasons behind the transmission of data to or between computer installations are rather different, however. As has been stressed many times previously in this book, the use of scientific management techniques, allied to the speed of modern computer processing, can provide management with a high degree of flexibility in its approach to problems, and hence allow very close control of a company's operations. It must be remembered that a computer merely computes and does not produce data; the data to be processed must travel from a source to the computer installation, and the processed data from the computer installation to a destination. If the time taken to transfer data to and from the computer installation is unduly long, some of the flexibility to be gained from the use of a computer may be lost. In many cases the data to be processed has its source near the computer installation, so that data transmission presents no problems; or the data may not need to be processed very urgently. The trend, however, is for management to require increasingly up to date information in order to obtain increasingly close control of the operations being managed. This leads logically to the use of on-line rather than off-line data transmission systems; that is to say, data is transferred from its source directly into the computer store rather than on to some intermediate medium which is subsequently input to the computer.

When a computer is initially installed in a company it is usually used at first for general accounting procedures, payroll, invoicing, sales ledger, and so on. Once these procedures have been successfully run on the computer for some time, management starts to look for more sophisticated ways of exploiting the computer's potential. The production division may, for instance, be able to benefit from computerized production control. This could involve a system whereby an input device is located at one end of a production line and output devices at each section further down the line. The input device could be a card reader, and the output devices simple printers. Production schedules are drawn up in advance on the computer, and a card punched with details of each unit to be produced. As production starts on a unit at one end of the line, the appropriate punched card is input to the card reader. The computer causes details of each type of component to be manufactured to be typed out on the output device in the section producing that component. In this way the production of individual components is closely controlled and an up to the minute record of exactly what has been used and produced is kept. The system could be further developed by extending input and output facilities on-line to the computer to other departments so that a completely up to date record is kept of the flow of all materials within the organization. In such a case management could be provided with typewriter terminals for inquiry purposes, in order to ascertain the exact state at any one moment of any of the jobs in progress.

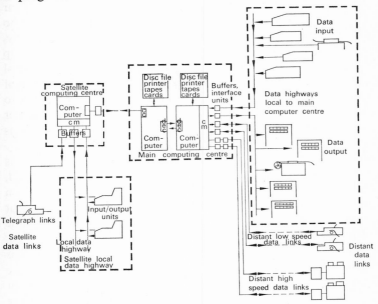

FIG. 48. Typical comprehensive computer controlled system incorporating data transmission.

In companies where production is carried out at a number of factories in different locations, a summary of details of each day's production output could be transmitted to a central computer installation; control of stocks at different points distant to the central computer installation could be dealt with in the same way. The summarized information is most likely to be transmitted off-line (Fig. 48). A tape would be punched with the summarized information each day, and transmitted by means of a paper tape reader connected to a telegraph or telephone line to the central computer installation. A corresponding tape would be punched at the computer installation by a tape punch connected to the same line. When all the tapes had been received they would be input to the computer to update production and inventory files and produce the required analyses.

As a company's use of data processing facilities grows, it may be decided to install punched-card equipment at various branches. The punched-card installations could handle small jobs of local significance; large jobs or information of relevance to the whole organization could be transmitted either on- or off-line to be processed at the central computer installation. Further expansion of the company's data processing effort may justify the installation of computers at some of the branches. The branch computers would then handle all local data processing and transmit only management information to the central computer. Finally, it may be decided to connect two or more of the computers by a permanent on-line link. The permanent link would allow work to be shared between the installations so as to avoid peak loads, and also provide a means of continuing work in the event of any one of the computers being temporarily out of action.

Data links in themselves are not costly; a telephone wire can be used for the same charge as that made to anyone making a normal telephone call. Permanent on-line facilities to distant points are more expensive; nevertheless, the cost of hardware generally is tending to decrease with technological developments and the increasing use of data processing equipment. It is thus possible to envisage at some future date the linking of all computers being used by a company into one large computing complex. The next step would be links between the computer complexes of different companies, and eventually possibly even a national network of data transmission and computer facilities.

Index